In Twenty-Five Words or Less...

THE COMPLETE GUIDE

TO WINNING CONTESTS

BY

Gloria Rosenthal

A FIRESIDE BOOK

PUBLISHED BY SIMON AND SCHUSTER

NEW YORK

Copyright © 1980 by Gloria Rosenthal
All rights reserved
including the right of reproduction
in whole or in part in any form
A Fireside Book
Published by Simon and Schuster
A Division of Gulf & Western Corporation
Simon & Schuster Building
Rockefeller Center
1230 Avenue of the Americas
New York, New York 10020
FIRESIDE and colophon
are trademarks of Simon & Schuster
Manufactured in the United States of America

1 2 3 4 5 6 7 8 9 10

Library of Congress Cataloging in Publication Data

Rosenthal, Gloria.
    In twenty-five words or less . . .

    (A Fireside book)
    1. Contests. I. Title.
GV1201.6.R67   790.1'34   80-13511

ISBN 0-671-25275-5

Twenty-Five Thanks...
or More

I feel like an Academy Award winner about to stammer out that there are so many people to thank I don't know where to begin.

Except I do know where; I have to begin with one person who must be thanked before all others—my sister Babe, also known as Dorothy Scott. Babe started me out in contesting, her winning entries are scattered throughout the book, and she wouldn't give me her entries until I promised her top billing.

Michael Donner, who is editor of *Games* magazine unknowingly started this whole project by asking me to write an article on contesting for *Games*. My editor, Barbara Jackson, saw the article and the potential, and told me I could write a book. Once the book was under way, Michael gave me all the help I needed from *Games*.

If I hadn't been coerced into thanking Babe first, I would have given that spot to Thomas J. Conlon, President of D. L. Blair, one of the finest judging agencies in the world. Tom gave me a great deal of time (which he doesn't have) and a great deal of advice (which I had to have) in the formative stages of this book, and I often found myself speaking in his voice. He proved over and over that judges are exceptionally nice people.

Other judges proved it, too: Jeffrey Feinman, President, Ventura Associates, Inc.; Don Jagoda, President,

5

National Judging Institute; William Murphy, President, V.I.P. Services, Inc.; and Richard Kane, President, Marden-Kane, Inc. They all took time to answer my questions and were never too busy to take my calls.

And speaking of judges (of another kind), my dear friend, Leonard L. Finz, a former Justice of the Supreme Court of the State of New York, answered all my legal questions.

Howard Doerr of the Shepherd School, and Roger and Carolyn Tyndall, publishers of *Contest News-Letter* were extremely cooperative. I knew I could call on them whenever I needed an entry or two to illustrate a point, and their bulletins were never out of my reach.

My children, Edward and Amy, earned my thanks way back when they were tiny tots uttering "bright sayings," some of which were turned into contest winners.

Lurline Berg, Norma Feuer, Marjorie Farley Goldberg, Tom Morris, Ellen Oseff, Sue Pollack, Lola Schancer, Elsye Wilson and several Anonymouses—winners all—gave their winning entries to the book. All of these entries were extremely important to me, and I appreciated having such good friends to call on.

My sister-in-law, Felice Golden, was always here when I needed her. She came to proofread and stayed to make many worthwhile suggestions.

When vacation time and deadlines clashed, I packed my bag, my work, and my husband and headed for Mohonk Mountain House in New Paltz, New York. Everyone up there recognized desperation when they saw it, and they gave me an office, a desk and a typewriter. For that, my thanks to all, and especially to Ben Matteson, Carolyn Fiske, and Jane Chase who let me share her office and who was tempted to scold me when I didn't come to work. I also have to thank the trout in Lake Mohonk for keeping husband Larry busy while I was working.

Another great place to write a book is at Whiffletree Campsites in Olive Bridge, New York. My understanding fellow campers called me a "woodpecker" instead of a nuisance as the tap, tap, tap of my typewriter broke the beautiful silence up there in the woods.

My thanks to a very special friend, Rick Atwell, who shares some of my projects and roots for all the others.

Ed Doty, a man who always found time for me and without whose help and expertise this book could never have been written deserves a special kind of thanks. So, thanks, Ed . . . for keeping my typewriter in repair.

And now we come to the backbone of it all—the group of people out there who make it all happen. A resounding thank you to all those sponsors who have ever run a contest, and to all those who have yet to run them; to all the companies who gave me permission to include entry blanks, winning entries, and pages from books and magazines. Sponsors are nice people, too. A special tribute to all the judging agencies and sponsors who have given me such wonderful prizes, and something always to look forward to, over the years. They're all partners in this book.

With love to Larry . . .
who never believed I could say anything
in twenty-five words . . . or less!

Contents

Foreword

It's not very gentlemanly to admit something like this in print, but I've been carrying on a love affair with Gloria Rosenthal for a great many years now. Not a very conventional love affair, I'll admit, but Gloria's not a very conventional gal.

The first time I met Gloria, she introduced herself as G. Rosenthal. Then she wanted to be called *Mrs.* G. Rosenthal. I figured our relationship was going nowhere when she suddenly insisted that I call her by her first name. I must have done something wrong, though, because five minutes later she demanded that I address her as Mrs. Lawrence Rosenthal. As the years passed and I got to know her better, I realized that these mercurial changes in persona were more than just a personal idiosyncrasy. Sometimes I'd encounter her three times in a single day. The first time she'd be Mrs. L. Rosenthal. Ten minutes later she'd be Ms. G. Rosenthal, and twenty minutes after that she'd be Gloria again! It was all very puzzling.*

Over the years, Gloria and I carried on a correspondence. I never told my wife, of course, but I think her husband knew. He was very twentieth-century about it, however. He never confronted me or asked Gloria to

---

* *Not so puzzling after you read Gloria's remarks on "keying" entries.*

break it off. Even when he discovered that I was occasionally sending her money.

Don't get me wrong, though, Gloria wasn't interested in me just for my money. She was perfectly happy to settle for a trip to Las Vegas or a new car. Depending on her mood, she could even be pleased by a refrigerator or excited by a washing machine. Funny gal, Gloria.

Now that I look back upon it, our correspondence was pretty unconventional, too. Gloria sent me an *awful* lot of letters. It would be indiscreet of me to quote from them, but for the most part they dealt with love and pleasure and desire. (Unfortunately for my ego, they dealt with love of toothpaste and spaghetti sauce, pleasure with floor polishers and detergents, and desire for prizes.)

My letters to Gloria were less frequent and considerably less imaginative. Nonetheless, I think they were exciting in their own way since they always began with the salutation: "Congratulations! I am pleased to announce that you have just won ..." Gloria, as you have undoubtedly guessed, was (and still is) an inveterate contester. More to the point, Gloria was so good at contests that she won with disturbing regularity.

My love affair with Gloria Rosenthal began when I first started judging contest entries and found that hers were consistently among the freshest and most creative sent in. And, *mirabile dictu!*, she followed the rules. Though I met Gloria more than a decade ago through her contest entries, I only met the lady in person when she began to research this book. To my delight, the G. Rosenthal who won so many of our contests was just as lovely, bright and charming as her entries.

I know of no contester who is more qualified than Gloria to write a book like this. Now that she has elevated herself to contest judge and pundit, perhaps I can begin to develop a new love affair with you, her reader.

Tom Conlon
President, D. L. Blair
Contest Judging Agency

Introduction

The year was 1961. I was recovering from major surgery. My husband was starting up the "executive ladder" in the frenetic world of advertising; we had two terrific, brilliant children (if you don't believe *me*, ask my husband); and there was nothing more I wanted out of life . . . except a dishwasher. No, scratch that. I didn't merely want one, I was *desperate* for one. I'll go even further. A dishwasher was a downright necessity if we were ever to hear the clink of silver against china again. You see, in order to save energy—my own, not the ecological kind —we used throwaway paper plates and vowed to buy a dishwasher *after* the doctor bills, drug bills, children's shoes, and the like. In the meantime, we bought more paper plates and cursed a budget that kept throwing its "wait!" around.

One afternoon, as I sipped soup from a soggy paper cup, the mail was delivered . . . and we were delivered! For there among the bills, the get-well cards, the junk mail, the postcard from a friend having a wonderful time, was the kind of letter I had come to recognize. With a remarkable display of strength for one who couldn't even wash a glass, I tore the envelope open, snatched the letter out, and found the glorious, longed-for words that seemed to jump off the page:

CONGRATULATIONS! . . . SECOND   PRIZE . . . DISHWASHER

For me, it was the fulfillment of several dreams.

I was a winner despite debilitating illness; I had my dishwasher; and it proved beyond doubt to all scoffers that I knew what I was doing. And what I was doing was entering contests as a hobby—a hobby we all had good reason to cheer many times. Even the children, young as they were, understood that "Mommy wins" meant they had the dolls, bikes, trains, mechanical robots we otherwise couldn't afford. Larry and I had the wristwatches, television sets, washer-dryer, radios, nights on the town, cash (no, the doctors got the cash). And speaking of cash, one of the prizes was an eighty-pound bag of silver dollars. You'll find out how much that is, and the entry that won it, if you just keep reading. Still to be won were more washing machines, dryers, dishwashers, ranges, carpeting, trips to Jamaica and Las Vegas . . . you name it.

I can remember vividly the precise moment I fell for this hobby, and became determined to join the ranks of consistent winners. My sister Babe had moved to Chicago where she joined a newcomer's club. There she met, and wrote to me about, a woman who had taken a correspondence course in contest winning, who subscribed to contest bulletins, who belonged to a National Contester's Association (a what?) and who, incredible as it seemed, was "always winning something." On the first day of my visit there, this unusual woman called Babe to report her latest prize—500 dollars. It seemed like a fortune back then, but it was the excitement in her voice more than the money (no, it was the money, too!) that turned Babe and me into immediate contest hobbyists. We pursued it with vigor, taking the course, subscribing to bulletins. I even found others in my area who were interested, and I formed the Queens Contest Club.

Six months later, I won my first prize and knew the thrill of winning with my words. My word, my words were working! Those judges picked my entry out of maybe hundreds of thousands of entries. True, they picked it for a last prize—it was a first aid kit, and I cut myself opening it—but no matter. That prize, still in the trunk of our car, was a treasure. I should tell you that beginning contesters are getting smarter and smarter. With the help of veteran contesters—and the kind of advice given in this book—they're winning bigger prizes in a lot less time.

For you, perhaps, this is the precise moment—that instant—when you picked up this book and thought, If *she* can do it, so can I (true!). Or perhaps it will come just a little bit later, when you learn the difference between skill contests and sweepstakes and understand there are tricks to the contesting trade, and the harder you work at anything (in this case fun), the better your accomplishments. But by the time you take the tests in this book, and discover that you *can* write a rhyme, create a slogan, cook up an unusual dish, you're sure to be hooked.

However, to be a real winner, you must first learn that "contesting" and "entering a contest" are not the same. There is a vast difference in attitude between the two activities.

"Entering a contest" is a haphazard affair. By chance you come across an entry blank which invites you to finish a statement in twenty-five words, or less. You write the first words that come to mind and send them in . . . with great expectations. Which is almost always wasted effort because thousands of people probably have written the very same words you did. Sounds impossible I know, but wait until you read about "duplicated entries" later in the book.

So much for entering a contest. What I want you to do is take up the hobby of contesting.

A hobby? Isn't a hobby something like photography, ceramics, stamp or coin collecting? Of course! They're fun, interesting, entertaining—and sometimes expensive. Contesting is a hobby, too. It's fun, interesting, entertaining—and often lucrative. Your single largest expense may very well be the cost of this book.

Other hobbies can be time-consuming and restrictive. You can't, for example, make a clay pot while waiting in the doctor's office. But you can use that time to write a limerick, and that's more satisfying than reading the doctor's three-year-old magazines. You can't do needlework in the shower, but you can think about why you like that particular brand of soap—and if they're running a contest, that's the brand of soap you should be using. Even while waiting for the traffic light to change, you can be mulling over a fresh, new way to say the same old thing.

The immediate rewards of contesting are obvious. There is the joy of creating and the thrill of winning. There are the many luxuries you might never have come by, but even if, for example, you could buy your own dishwasher, winning it because you know *how* to win it is . . . well, look at it this way: Writing an entry is much more gratifying than writing a check. The next reward is something you won't think about until you start entering in earnest, and that is the anticipation, the looking forward to something every single day, the running to get the mail because who knows what good news and prizes it will bring.

In my case, there was (and still is) another reward I could never have imagined back there in Chicago when the contest bug took a big bite out of me. As a direct result of contesting, my skill with words began improving rapidly. My entries were getting better. My prizes were getting bigger. I was selling more major appliances that I couldn't use than Friendly Frost. And I was thinking of branching out (in my writing, not my selling). Two of my contesting friends had already channeled their love of words into taking a course in etymology (the study of words), and I joined them. As a class, we researched and wrote *A Play on Words* which was published by Macmillan in 1969.

Of course, we kept our hand in contesting, and no matter how busy we were writing the book, all we had to do was hear "Finish this statement . . . ," and we were off and running like the old fire dog who hears the sound of the alarm.

When the book was finished, I wanted to do more. I

began to teach myself writing for the freelance market, and discovered that many of the same techniques I had employed for my entries were the same techniques I needed to write fillers, light verse, greeting cards, even fiction and articles. I went from twenty-five words to one thousand to ten thousand (some magazines pay by the word!) to writing this book.

All right, I have to say it though I hesitate: Contesting also taught me that you "can't win 'em all," so I was able to accept rejections without taking them as a personal attack. Anyhow, I always figured a writer has so many rejections in a lifetime, and I was just getting mine out of the way early. That's how I convinced myself that every rejection was taking me that much closer to an acceptance.

And I was right. My material was beginning to meet with approval, just as my entries had after a short while. I was selling (not appliances but my writing), and I decided to teach others what I had learned. I called my adult education course "Writing To Be Published," and many of my students in the Hewlett-Woodmere School District on Long Island have gone on to do just that.

My writing seemed to be getting a bit off the contesting course, although I still never missed an opportunity to enter one. Then, a brand-new magazine named *Games* was published. I began to read it with a contester's eye, since they were running several types in every issue. Soon, I was reading it with a writer's eye. Since they were running contests, maybe I could create and judge some for them.

When I went to see Michael Donner, who is editor of *Games*, I brought along my complete book of contest entries (winners and losers because they're all important as you'll soon find out). Mike saw the book, asked me to write an article on my hobby, told me I could create and judge contests, and a short time later made me a Contributing Editor and Contest Administrator.

From there, this book was born.

All this because my sister moved to Chicago!

And now this book is your "Chicago." This is where you will learn that every contester has the potential to become a consistent winner *if* . . .

If you read every page, study every rule, apply every technique (even this sentence is a technique—see Mystic Three, page 46), you might be taking that first step on the road that could lead to a trip to Europe for completing a jingle, a mobile home for naming a puppy, 25,000 dollars for twenty-five simple words.

Or a career in freelance writing? A spot as a contributing editor on a national magazine? Who knows? I surely didn't when I sent out my first entry with such determination and, to this day, don't know what is yet to come. My mail hasn't arrived yet, and there are three big contests about to break. Who knows . . . ?

Before you go on please read these important suggestions which will help you get the most out of this book.

Please write in this book! Yes, read it with pencil in hand, because you will come across portions called *Your Turn,* which will be your turn to test the knowledge you're acquiring. Want to underline a phrase, or make notes in the margin? Do it. This is your book to learn from, scribble in, refer to, and not the kind of book you should lend out, anyhow. Let your friends buy their own.

Contest entries used throughout to illustrate winning techniques are, indeed, winning entries and are reproduced exactly as they were submitted, capital letters, quotes, underlining, and all. That way you will see exactly how a prize-winning entry was presented. Whenever nonwinners are used—either for comparison or to test your ability to judge—the actual winners will be revealed by chapter's end, if not before.

Now, if you're anxious to get on with this, to turn the page, to learn more, to apply that knowledge, go to it— and go get 'em!

1

Learning the Lingo

Everybody knows what rules are, but in contesting we will go one step further in defining them. The rules you find on an Official Entry Blank are written in cement; they are made *not* to be broken, or even chipped away. So Lesson One is simple: OBEY THE RULES!

Paste this phrase on your shaving or makeup mirror; tape it to your refrigerator; write it one hundred times or more! Do whatever you must to make it as much a part of entering every contest as licking a postage stamp. Never, and I don't mean hardly ever, but *never* enter any contest without first studying the rules for that contest. Yes, I said *studying.* I didn't say read the rules because reading can lead to skimming and skimming can lead to oversights. Sure, it's tempting to skip some of the fine print, especially if the rules start out just like other contests you've entered, and you assume they will be exactly the same.

Lesson Two: NEVER ASSUME ANYTHING! Contest rules are written to give every contestant an equal opportunity to submit a winning entry. If you think you can outwit your competition by bending the rules even a bit, remember that the judge knows what those rules are, and he not only *won't* break them for your brilliant (of course!) entry, but he *can't* by law. So if the rules ask for twenty-five words, let there not be twenty-six. And if a

25

number 10 business envelope is called for, don't think you can make your entry stand out in a 9 x 12 manila envelope. Oh, it will stand out all right—out in the trash can. If you are told to sign your entry, it's because they want your signature, not your typing or your printing.

What you must always remember is that entry blanks are not just a string of words. They are well thought out, clearly expressed, easily understood directions that must be taken seriously and verbatim. It would be unfair and illegal for judges to make exceptions.

At the end of this chapter, you will find sample entry blanks with each rule analyzed and explained. It seems elementary, but at least 20 percent of all entries in national contests are discarded because one simple rule or another was not adhered to. Don't lose a contest for a reason like that.

You've just learned one of the most important lessons in this book, and it will be repeated throughout since it applies to every kind of prize promotion you will encounter.

WHAT'S A PRIZE PROMOTION?

Advertising promotions offering prizes are called, appropriately enough, prize promotions. Two such promotions are skill contests, where some form of writing is required, and sweepstakes (or drawings), where nothing is written but a name and address. Although they are lumped together as contests, there are important distinctions that the serious contester should understand.

In skill contests, you will be required to demonstrate, as the name implies, your skill at completing a sentence, composing a last line, creating a name, slogan, title . . . whatever. Your entry will be judged on the basis of what you have created. In such a contest, the sponsor can, and usually does, ask that you purchase his product in order to enter his contest. He can insist that a proof of that purchase, in the form of box top, label, wrapper, or the like, be enclosed with your entry. If you leave it out, your entry will be thrown out. (Remember, read those rules!) In contest lingo, the proof of purchase is known as a "qualifier" since it qualifies your entry. In lazy lingo, the qualifier becomes a "qualie."

Sponsors of sweepstakes can make no such demands on their entrants. They can't insist on proof of purchase because your entry will not be judged but picked (you hope!) at random, which involves nothing more than chance. If you were asked to pay a price (make a purchase), the sweeps would actually become a lottery with the sponsor "selling" you a ticket for the price of his product. And that's illegal. Now, sponsors often *ask* for a proof of purchase, but down there in that fine print (which you will be reading, right?), you will always find a free alternative. This alternative, writing the name of the product on a slip of paper, for instance, will qualify your entry just as if you had bought the product and enclosed the label. Don't make the mistake of thinking you can improve your chances of winning by sending the label. The judge must obey his own rules, and it would be highly illegal for the judging agency to favor an entrant for any reason whatsoever.

A JUDGING AGENCY—WHAT'S THAT?

Sponsors of national contests don't do their own judging. They turn to judging agencies, companies totally experienced and fully equipped to cope with the hundreds of problems and thousands of entries involved in prize promotions. Entry blanks include the name of the judging agency, along with the criteria by which the entries will be judged, which is most helpful *if* the contestant knows how to take advantage of such information. And that's where judging slant comes in.

JUDGING SLANT—DOES IT EXIST?

Judges say, "No!" Every judge I interviewed insisted there was no such thing as writing (or "slanting") your entry to appeal to a particular judging agency. A few admitted that this was not always true, that years ago you could be sure that one agency favored puns; another went for the straight-talk type of entry; and still another gave the nod to rhymed entries. In those days, entry blanks did not include judging criteria. Today, the judges view your entries with a very structured point system in mind, for example 50 percent for originality, 25 percent for clarity, 15 percent for aptness of thought, and so on. In some cases, the percentages may be omitted, but the rules will still say that judging is based on such specifics as clarity, creativity, appropriateness for advertising purposes, or whatever the advertiser deems important to the subject matter. Even so, after you've been contesting for a while and winning from the same judges, you may assume you are pleasing them with your style. Certainly, if an agency always lists creativity at 60 percent, you would know that clever entries, as opposed to straightforward ones, do, indeed, rate high in that office, and you would strive for that cleverness in your entries.

Once you decide to try slanting, you must learn the tricks of this particular trade. How will you know which entry won the prize when you've sent in several to one contest? The sponsor won't tell you; the judging agency won't tell you; the lovely letter of congratulations will only tell you *what* you've won but not *how* you won. Ah, but there is a clue, and the way the winning letter was addressed is the key to your winning entry.

KEYING YOUR ENTRIES

Keying is a method used by advertisers when they want to know which advertising medium is doing the best job for them. When an ad includes some kind of mail-in coupon, they use a code in the address, or as they say in the ad biz, they "key it." If the coupon appears, for example, in *Games* magazine, that coupon will have Dept. G (or GM) as part of the address. The same ad running in *The New York Times* would read Dept. NYT. They can go one step further and find out which issue of a publication pulled the best by keying with the month as well. All they have to do is add the month after the letters and they have a keying for the September issue of *McCall's* that will look like this: Dept. MC9—or *McCall's,* ninth month.

You are going to do the same thing with your entries, but because you can't fool around with your address, you will do so with your name. You will give each entry in the *same* contest a variation of your name and then keep a record of how you sent the entries in. Let's say Amy Beth Edwards is married to Lawrence Steve Edwards. The variations of her name are almost endless: Amy Edwards, Amy Beth Edwards, A. B. Edwards, A. Beth Edwards, Mrs. L. S. Edwards, Mrs. Larry Edwards, Mr. L. Steve Edwards, and so on and so on. She will run out of ideas before she will run out of names. The important key to keying is, of course, good record keeping. More about that in Chapter 11. A few successes from a particular judge may reveal preferences, and you can slant future entries with this knowledge in mind.

BLACKLISTING—WHY IT DOESN'T EXIST

About now, you must be worrying that a judge will see your name again and again and decide you've won enough already. Maybe he would like to give someone else a chance, but it would be illegal for him to do so. If you follow all the rules and write the best entry, you will win the prize. The entry, not the entrant, is being judged. If a judge were to let his personal feelings interfere with his professional judgment, he would be guilty of breaking the law just as surely as if he had stolen from you which, in effect, he would be doing. Some agencies remove name and address and send coded entries to the senior judges; some don't. But either way, you are assured of an impartial reading and fair evaluation. Contests are highly regulated and any hanky-panky would come under the ominous heading of a Federal offense. It's not nice to use the mails to defraud.

No reputable sponsor or judging agency would risk the wrath of Uncle Sam just so a cousin could win a prize.

SO ALL CONTESTS ARE HONEST, RIGHT?

Wrong. *Most* contests are honest, especially national contests using the mails, which are regulated by the government. Certainly, there are some (but not all) local contests where entries are dropped into a drum, as opposed to being mailed, and a local merchant, not quite as blindfolded as he should be, may pick a winner. I'm not making any accusations, nor am I saying they are surely fixed. I'm just noting the possibility. These contests might be worth a shot if you don't put too much effort into the entry, or if they are sweepstakes, or if they are not taking time away from a more important prize promotion. I, personally, prefer the mail-in variety because then I know the government is looking over my judge's shoulder, which gives me a nice sense of security. Incidentally, this is another reason why contests are so legitimate and you can win over and over again. If called upon by the government, judging agencies must justify their selection of winners. They cannot award a prize to just anyone if the entry does not meet all of the judging criteria listed in the rules.

In any event, sour grapes make sour contestants, and every contest you lose is not fixed. You have to trust your instincts sometimes and learn not to be cynical, but devote most of your efforts to those promotions that seem to be the most reliable.

In addition to national contests, there are many radio, television, magazine and newspaper competitions that are fairly judged and great fun to enter.

ANATOMY OF AN ENTRY BLANK
(SWEEPSTAKES)

1. *Official Entry Blank or plain piece of 3-inch x 5-inch paper:* There are no other choices. Plain means unlined and unadorned. Buy a 3 x 5 pad and keep it handy for sweepstakes.

2. *Hand print your name and address:* Do not write. Do not type.

3. *Hand-addressed envelope:* May be handwritten or printed but not typed.

4. *No larger than 4⅛ inches x 9½ inches:* A #10 envelope is the long, white business envelope. The way this rule is written, your envelope can be smaller but not larger.

5. *Label:* Must be from product specified—in this case, *any size* will do. Sending label from largest size *cannot* increase your chances, or rules would have to state that (and in a sweeps it would be against the law).

6. *"EVERYNIGHT SHAMPOO" hand printed:* Hand printed (not written), exactly as specified, in caps with quotes. Quotes may not be necessary but put them in just in case. This is as good as a label!

7. *Plain piece of 3-inch x 5-inch paper:* Go back to Number 1, above.

8. *Each entry must be mailed separately:* If you put in two to save postage, you've wasted postage. Follow those rules!

9. *Received by . . .* means exactly that: If your entry arrives even one day late, nobody will see it but the trash collector. With our postal system, allow plenty of time for entry to be received—a minimum of seven days from coast to coast. (Sounds crazy, but you know our postal system.)

Anatomy of an Entry Blank—Sweepstakes

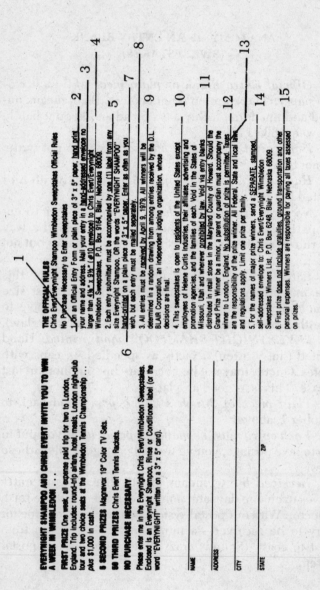

EVERYNIGHT SHAMPOO AND CHRIS EVERT INVITE YOU TO WIN A WEEK IN WIMBLEDON . . .

FIRST PRIZE One week, all expense paid trip for two to London, England. Trip includes: round-trip airfare, hotel, meals, London night-club tour and two choice seats at the Wimbledon Tennis Championship . . . Plus $1,000 in cash.

6 SECOND PRIZES Magnavox 19" Color TV Sets.

60 THIRD PRIZES Chris Evert Tennis Rackets.

NO PURCHASE NECESSARY

Please enter me in the Everynight Chris Evert/Wimbledon Sweepstakes. Enclosed is an Everynight Shampoo, Rinse or Conditioner label (or the word "EVERYNIGHT" written on a 3" x 5" card).

NAME _____

ADDRESS _____

CITY _____

STATE _____ ZIP

THE OFFICIAL RULES
Chris Evert/Everynight Shampoo Wimbledon Sweepstakes Official Rules
No Purchase Necessary to Enter Sweepstakes

1. On an Official Entry Form or plain piece of 3" x 5" paper, hand print your name and address. Mail your entry in a hand-addressed envelope no larger than 4¼" x 9½" (#10 envelope) to Chris Evert/Everynight Wimbledon Sweepstakes, P.O. Box 9164, Blair, Nebraska 68009.

2. Each entry submitted must be accompanied by one (1) label from any size Everynight Shampoo, OR the words "EVERYNIGHT SHAMPOO" hand-printed on a plain piece of 3" x 5" paper. Enter as often as you wish, but each entry must be mailed separately.

3. All entries must be received by April 9, 1979. All winners will be determined in a random drawing from among entries received by the D.L. BLAIR Corporation, an independent judging organization, whose decisions are final.

4. This sweepstakes is open to residents of the United States except employees of Helene Curtis Industries, their affiliates, advertising and promotion agencies, and the families of each. Void in the States of Missouri, Utah and wherever prohibited by law. Void via entry blanks distributed in retail stores in the Maryland County of Howard. Should the Grand Prize Winner be a minor, a parent or guardian must accompany the winner to London, England. No substitution of prize is permitted. Taxes are the responsibility of the prize winner. All Federal, State and local laws and regulations apply. Limit one prize per family.

5. For the names of major prize winners, send a SEPARATE, stamped, self-addressed envelope to: Chris Evert/Everynight Wimbledon Sweepstakes Winners List, P.O. Box 6248, Blair, Nebraska 68009.

6. First prize does not include gratuities, ground transportation and other personal expenses. Winners are responsible for paying all taxes assessed on prizes.

Entry blank reprinted through courtesy of the D. L. Blair Corporation

10. *Sweepstakes open to . . . except . . . :* If you don't qualify, don't bother.

11. *Void in the state of . . . :* If you live in Utah, sorry about that. Also check other restrictions, depending on where you live.

12. *No substitution of prizes:* If you really can't use it, or sell it, save your time. If they say no, it's no.

13. *Taxes:* Yes, you have a partner—Uncle Sam. More about that in Chapter 11.

14. *Winner's list:* If you want the winner's list, don't include your request with your entry. See that great, big SEPARATE?

15. *First Prize does not include . . . :* Always check to see what you may win before you enter. You might not want the vacation if you have to pay your air fare. (Doesn't apply in this case but something to watch out for.)

Even one broken rule will disqualify you. It is estimated that at least 20 percent of all entrants do not follow the rules. Make sure you're not in that category. Make it a habit to check everything before you seal the envelope.

ANATOMY OF AN ENTRY BLANK
(SKILL CONTEST)

1. *Complete the last three lines:* Don't think one or two lines will be acceptable. They want a limerick so you *must* write a limerick. If you can't, you will learn how in Chapter 3.

2. *Follow the rules:* Now, isn't that what I've been trying to tell you!

3. *Entry form or plain paper no larger than 8½ x 11 (one side only):* Nothing left to the imagination here. A good judging agency spells it out very clearly. Heed them well! And be sure to write on one side only.

4. *Hand print:* I mean, be sure to HAND PRINT on one side only! (No writing or typing.)

Anatomy of an Entry Blank—Skill Contests

OFFICIAL ENTRY FORM

To enter the "Flick My Bic" Limerick Contest, complete the last three lines of this limerick and follow the rules on the back of this form:

"I once knew a pretty good trick,
that began with a 'Flick of My Bic'

_____

_____

"

_____

Fill in your name and address (print plainly).

Mail your completed entry blank with PROOF-OF-PURCHASE (the words "Bic Lighter" cut from the front of the Bic Lighter Package) to: "Flick My Bic" Contest, P.O. Box 9186, Blair, Nebraska 68009.

Name
_____

Address
_____

City, State, Zip
_____

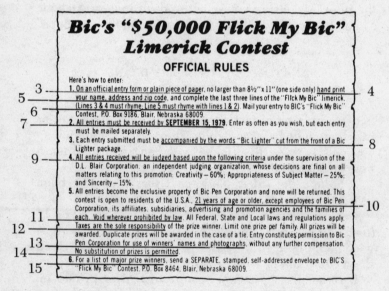

Bic's "$50,000 Flick My Bic" Limerick Contest

OFFICIAL RULES

Here's how to enter:

1. On an official entry form or plain piece of paper, no larger than 8½" x 11" (one side only) hand print your name, address and zip code, and complete the last three lines of the "Flick My Bic" limerick. (Lines 3 & 4 must rhyme; Line 5 must rhyme with lines 1 & 2). Mail your entry to BIC's "Flick My Bic" Contest, P.O. Box 9186, Blair, Nebraska 68009.

2. All entries must be received by SEPTEMBER 15, 1979. Enter as often as you wish, but each entry must be mailed separately.

3. Each entry submitted must be accompanied by the words "Bic Lighter" cut from the front of a Bic Lighter package.

4. All entries received will be judged based upon the following criteria under the supervision of the D.L. Blair Corporation, an independent judging organization, whose decisions are final on all matters relating to this promotion: Creativity — 60%; Appropriateness of Subject Matter — 25%; and Sincerity — 15%.

5. All entries become the exclusive property of Bic Pen Corporation and none will be returned. This contest is open to residents of the U.S.A., 21 years of age or older, except employees of Bic Pen Corporation, its affiliates, subsidiaries, advertising and promotion agencies and the families of each. Void wherever prohibited by law. All Federal, State and Local laws and regulations apply. Taxes are the sole responsibility of the prize winner. Limit one prize per family. All prizes will be awarded. Duplicate prizes will be awarded in the case of a tie. Entry constitutes permission to Bic Pen Corporation for use of winners' names and photographs, without any further compensation. No substitution of prizes is permitted.

6. For a list of major prize winners, send a SEPARATE, stamped, self-addressed envelope to: BIC'S "Flick My Bic" Contest, P.O. Box 8464, Blair, Nebraska 68009.

Entry blank reprinted through the courtesy of the D. L. Blair Corporation

5. *Name, address and zip code:* Since they ask for the zip, be sure to include it. If you forget it . . . forget it!

6. *Lines 3 & 4 must rhyme; line 5 must rhyme with lines 1 & 2:* They're telling you exactly what you should do. Do it. If they wanted a different rhyming pattern, they would have asked for it.

7. *Received by . . . , each entry mailed separately:* Get those entries out separately and on time. And remember those postal delays.

8. *The words "BIC lighter" cut from the front . . . :* Since this is a skill contest, you *must* send in the qualifier requested, and it must be the exact portion of the wrapper asked for. Leave it out and you're out.

9. *Judging based on the following criteria:*
CREATIVITY gets a whopping 60 percent, which leaves plenty of room for originality, cleverness and—well—creativity. Trite entries won't win this one.

APPROPRIATENESS OF SUBJECT MATTER: Remember, you're talking about a cigarette lighter and a pretty good trick that started with the flick of it. Stick to the subject. Don't go too far afield in your effort to be original. Other contests, of course, will require other degrees of appropriateness, but stick to the subject. That's what aptness (and appropriateness) is all about, and you need that 25 percent in your score.

SINCERITY: They're going to give you 15 percent if you don't make up something so totally outlandish that it can't possibly be believed. Walk that fine line between creativity and sincerity with care. We'll soon show you how.

10. *21 years of age or older:* Be prepared to prove it if you win. Usual restrictions on employees or anyone connected with the parent company are also checkable.

11. *Void where prohibited:* A catch-all phrase meaning if you live in one of those difficult states, check it out . . . or move.

12. *Taxes:* Uncle Sam again; he's your partner.

13. *Use of winners' names and photographs:* Don't expect to get anything extra for such use. You enter the contest, you accept the rules.

Entry blank reprinted through the courtesy of The Paddington Corporation

PLANTERS® 'GO NUTS' CONTEST OFFICIAL RULES AND ENTRY FORM

Name _____ Address _____

City _____ State _____ Zip _____ Phone _____
(Required)

Store Name
Where Purchased _____ Address _____

City _____ State _____

Here's how to enter:

1. On an official entry form or on a plain piece of 3" x 5" paper, hand print your name, address and zip code, and store name and address where you purchased your Planters Nuts. On a separate piece of plain paper, tell us in twenty-five (25) words or less "How You 'Go Nuts' Outdoors with Planters." Example: "My friends and I 'Go Nuts' at five thousand feet! When sky-diving, we snack on Planters Nuts before we pull the cord."

Enclose one proof of purchase from any size can or jar of Planters Nuts (jar label or Mr. Peanut from yellow can lid). OR one empty bag of any size Southern Belle Nuts. OR three small bags or wrappers of any Planters Nuts.

Mail to: **Planters Go Nuts Contest**
P.O. Box 977
Young America, MN 55399

2. Enter as often as you wish, but each entry must be mailed separately. All entries must be postmarked by August 15, 1979 and received no later than August 31, 1979.

3. Winners will qualify on the basis of completing steps one and two above: Judging will be conducted on the following points:

1. Clarity of words used.
2. Appropriateness for use in advertising and promotion as they pertain to the image of Planters.
3. Originality and creativity.
All decisions of the judges will be final.

4. One grand prize winner: 1979 Chevrolet Corvette; 10 second prize winners: Coleman Camping Package; 25 third prize winners: Sony Swivelvision TV Plus "The Chair"; 2,000 fourth prize winners: 'Go Nuts' Duffle Bag. Winners must pay all applicable taxes. No substitution or transfer of prizes.

5. Contest open to all residents of the U.S. except for employees and their immediate families of Standard Brands, Inc., its advertising and its judging agencies.

6. All entries submitted become the exclusive property of Planters and none will be returned. All contest entrants grant all rights of reproduction of their entries in any form. Contest valid except where prohibited or restricted by law. The winners will be notified by mail on or before October 1, 1979. No correspondence will be entered into.

PLT 1060

Courtesy of PLANTERS, a division of Standard Brands Incorporated.

14. *No substitutions:* No substitutions, can't be clearer than that.

15. *Winner's list:* If you want one, send a separate, stamped, self-addressed envelope (an SASE in contest lingo).

YOUR TURN TO ANALYZE A SWEEPS

Time for you to practice what I teach. On page 36 is an entry blank for you to study. Read it over with the previous points in mind. And whenever you come upon a new contest, study each rule.

YOUR TURN TO ANALYZE A SKILL

As with sweeps, every rule counts—and in skill contests, every word counts, too. Analyze the rules (see page 37) just the way I did for you.

2
Making a Statement

Statement contests come in all sizes, from the short, familiar twenty-five words all the way up to the five-hundred-word essay. The short one is familiar because it is the one most often used by companies sponsoring statement contests. It is also, perhaps, the most formidable for the newcomer to contestland since it appears so deceptively simple. After all, you don't have to write a rhyme; you don't have to create a clever name or tricky slogan. All you have to do is tell the sponsor what he already knows about his product and convince him that you know it, too. If you can add a new twist, so much the better. It's as simple as that. Or is it?

IT'S NOT THAT SIMPLE—PART 1

Most people think it *is* that simple so they write the first thought that comes to mind which is, mostly, the first thought that comes to a lot of minds at the same time. No good. The most effective way to overcome the copycat entry is to take your first thoughts and write them down. Then throw them away. *Now* you are ready to get to work.

Think about the product. Really think about it. Study the advertising; read the complete box or label. Compare it, in your mind, to similar products you've used. If there really is something special about the contest brand, make a note of it. If you have some personal reason for preferring the brand, make a note of that. I once won with a highly personal idea in a DIAL soap contest. I had a temporary medical problem and could not use deodorants. That fact appeared in my entry. Even if there isn't anything special, you can find something to write about. If it's soap, sniff it. If it's ketchup, think about it while you're pouring it on. Make a mental note of the taste as you bite into your hamburger. Make those products live in your mind. Still can't find anything unique? Not to worry. You can still make your entry stand out by writing up the product's common virtues in an uncommon way. Which brings us to . . .

IT'S NOT THAT SIMPLE—PART 2

Most people write the way they talk, but "talking" your entry just isn't good enough. Your statement must be unique enough to be outstanding, yet simple enough to be believed. The line between the two can be tricky, but you will learn how to accomplish this balance, and when you combine your own thoughts with these proven techniques, you will be on your way to packing punch and potency into your sentence.

A SINGLE SENTENCE?

Yes. One sentence. The single-sentence structure is usually a must in short-statement contests. In most cases, the lead-in (the portion of the entry supplied by the sponsor) is the beginning of the sentence, and you will be instructed by the rules of the contest to "Finish this sentence [or statement] in twenty-five words, or less." *Finish this sentence* . . . Most beginners don't pay much attention to that phrase, and they write two or three sentences without realizing what they're doing.

What they're doing is breaking at least one rule that we know of, for sure, a rule that is easy to follow because —again—there are techniques which permit you to convey several different thoughts in one sentence while remaining grammatically correct—techniques like dashes —dots . . . semi-colons; all handy little tools to help you say what you want while sticking to the single-sentence structure.

Please reread that paragraph. Notice anything? If you realized there are no periods, you may have also noticed that all the techniques mentioned were employed to write all sixty-seven words in one sentence. Twenty-five is a snap.

An example of that technique in action follows. The sponsor's lead-in is in italics; the rest is the winning entry. *I serve my children school-day breakfasts of good hot QUAKER OATS because* . . . we're all magicians at breakfast—I make QUICK, nourishing, appealing QUAKER OATS appear in ONE MINUTE; the children make it disappear in "seconds." (Entry won bicycle.)

If you analyze this entry, you will see that I said nothing unusual about the product, but I did give the common that uncommon twist. Although I used QUICK as an adjective I capitalized it because on the box it appears as part of the product name. I also capitalized ONE MINUTE because that's how long it takes to cook QUAKER OATS, and with something as simple as the shift key on my typewriter I proved my knowledge of the product. Additionally, the word "seconds" can be taken two ways —the children eat it quickly, and they want a second helping.

Another important feature is the follow-through. When the sponsor gives such a particularized lead-in, rather than the vague, "I like [name of product] because . . . ," *always* follow that lead. In this case, breakfast was mentioned, so an entry stressing that QUAKER OATS makes a great meat loaf would have nothing to do with the subject and your "appropriateness to the subject" score would pull your entry way down. If you can work in an additional benefit you may do so, but it's not always possible to say all you want within the word count. Following the sponsor's lead takes priority.

Incidentally, the rules for this contest allowed the use of a facsimile. I submitted six entries: two with labels, four with facsimiles (hand-drawn reproductions). The above winner was entered with a facsimile and let me assure you, I'm no artist.

So, after you study your product, and after you make notes of its virtues and your preferences, and after you understand you must write a single sentence, you are well on your way to finishing that statement with twenty-five terrific words.

HOW ABOUT TWENTY-SIX TERRIFIC WORDS?

Forget it. Remember that rule to obey the rules? Follow it. There are two phrases that should be popping out of these pages by now: finish this sentence . . . twenty-five words or less. I've already told you that the word limit is an absolute. Now I want to be more specific. You'd be surprised to learn how many people think an extra word or two won't matter. Maybe you would not be surprised; maybe you are one of those who think the judges would not be that particular. They not only would be, but by law must be. If even one judge lets even one twenty-six-word statement win a prize, he would be guilty of breaking the law as well as breaking his own rules, and cheating every one of those contestants who obey them. However, just as you've already learned it's possible to stick to one sentence, so you will now discover that staying within the word limit is possible, if you work at it. And working at it merely means concentrating on what you're trying to say and getting your thoughts across in as few words as possible. This will automatically add two pluses to your entry; you will be able to pack important points into your statement, and you will score high on "conciseness," which means getting right to the point without rambling. It also means you are using as few words as possible to say what you want to say. Now, don't misconstrue that to mean you should try to use fewer than the twenty-five words allotted (although you certainly may); rather, it means to be comprehensive: to fill your statement with important, not idle, words. Conciseness is frequently found in the rules as part of the judging standards.

Unimportant words, the words that do nothing to enhance your statement and enchant your judge, must be eliminated. An excellent example of getting rid of useless wordage is the phrase, "I don't like," which consists of . . . how many words? Three? Well, *some* judges count it as three, but others might count contractions as two words, making "I don't like" add up to four. If you want to be safe, you will always count contractions as two words. Better to be under than over. Now, without altering the phrase's meaning, we can lop off two words. Instead of saying, "I don't like," say, "I dislike." Same meaning, different word count. Concise and to the point.

I gave you this example, but now it's your turn. The following phrases are listed along with their correct word count. The challenge here is for you to revise these phrases, reduce the word count, and keep the original meaning totally intact. The answers, given on page 67 under the heading, Your Turn—answers, are really answers. They're just basically examples. You may, and undoubtedly will, come up with excellent rewrites of your own. Don't be discouraged if your choices are different from mine. That's the whole point of contesting as a hobby. You can learn the techniques, but it isn't a science; what you do with the knowledge is a highly individual and personal matter. And because of these differences, your entries will not be carbon copies of those written by others who make the same study of it. It's your own mind making these tips work for you.

YOUR TURN

PHRASE AND WORD COUNT	YOUR REVISION AND WORD COUNT
1. I can't wait (4)	_____
2. I'm going to give (5)	_____
3. I like the taste of [Product name] (6 or more depending on number of words in product name)	_____
4. In spite of (3)	_____
5. Full of flavor (3)	_____
6. Pretty as a picture (4)	_____

Another method of cutting word count is the I-N-G ending. In other types of writing, the *ing* ending has a weakening effect. If you say, "I was running," it is not as strong as saying "I ran." If you say, as many beginning writers do, "Coming through the door, I saw a stranger," you've made a much weaker statement than if you had said, "I came through the door and saw a stranger." However, these same *ing* endings work for instead of against you when writing contest material. Take the two sentences below:

I like SNOW CROP because . . . when I eat breakfast I find that SNOW CROP . . .
I like SNOW CROP because . . . eating breakfast I find that SNOW CROP . . .

The second method lopped off two unimportant words which you may need later on in your statement to say something positively brilliant.

This device is used frequently by the regular contester who seldom wastes words by using the personal pronoun. Another example:

My favorite young fashion shoe is FOOT FLAIRS be-

cause . . . stressing smartness through simplicity, Foot Flairs' classic styles "tone-up" my wardrobe, contributing sound-support and youthful grace in easy-going fashion. (Entry won Foot Flair shoes, of course.)

Now that you've learned to count words, it's time to make words count. Again, I want to point out that you will be saying what everybody else is saying so you have to say it better, especially in those cases where your choice of the contest brand is not a highly motivated choice. Maybe you use BRILLO because your mother always did. Well, that could win in a contest if you write it up cleverly enough, adding sales points along the way (telling *why* your mother chose it and seeing no reason to switch). Still, there will be times when you're using a product just for the contest. In those cases, always try to give yourself time to use and become familiar with it before writing your entry. You will find, as I often do, that buying a contest brand will lead to lifelong loyalty. I'm still using 4C Bread Crumbs after buying it for a contest many years ago. I was impressed with it and wrote a winning entry.

The point is, no matter what point you're making, you must express yourself in a way that will make your entry sing; make your entry stand out in the crowd. Remember that the "crowd" will be duplicating each other all over the place, but you will be using specific contest devices to achieve . . . perhaps greatness.

CONTEST DEVICES—IN GENERAL

Now we're getting down to the nitty gritty of actually writing that statement, and we want that entry to have a flow, a sense of balance, a sense of specialness that will delight the judge. Incidentally, all the devices discussed here will apply, in varying degrees, to every kind of contest, so learn them well. Later on in this chapter you will find *The Winner Sanctum*, entries with notes pointing out what devices were used, and *Anatomy of an Entry*, showing how a First Prize Winner was created. This will utimately help you create your own entries because it will show you exactly how devices like Alliteration and Mystic Three, for example, were used successfully.

ALLITERATION AND MYSTIC THREE

These two devices are often seen together. Fowler's *Dictionary of Modern English Usage* says that alliteration is: "the purposive use in a phrase or sentence of words beginning with or containing the same letter or sound." Examples from that source include: "After life's *f*itful *f*ever; in a *s*ummer *s*eason when *s*oft was the *s*un."

This repetition of sound makes for pleasing and memorable phrases. Some such, which have become very familiar with constant use, are: safe and sound, hale and hearty, wax and wane, fickle finger of fate.

Again, we get back to the flow, the balance, of the words in your entry. Remember, you're not merely writing a sentence, you are *c*reatively *c*ompeting in a *c*ontest (get that alliteration!), and you are truly "making a statement." Your sentence must compare favorably with that of your competition, and you give your entry its best shot by thinking about your words and making each word used a part of the total effect. Alliteration adds to that effect.

Caution: Some sentences seem silly when sounds and syllables are supplied without some sense of sincerity . . . see? *Don't overdo!*

Mystic Three is a phrase coined by Wilmer S. Shepherd, founder of the Shepherd School, and author of the *Shepherd Coaching Course in Contest Winning* (more about that later). He used it to define any interesting trio of words or phrases. As you will see from the following overly familiar and non-contesty trios, Alliteration often plays an important part in making these trios pleasing to the ear:

> cool, calm and collected
> bewitched, bothered and bewildered

> stop, look and listen
> high, wide and handsome

"High and wide" employs similar sound while "high and handsome" relies on the repetition of consonants.

Mystic Three can also stand on its own, without the additional device of alliteration, as you will see from many of the winning entries in this book, but the sense of balance is still there.

The following winner is a good example of these two devices in action:

> A *REMINGTON Electric Shaver is an ideal gift because* . . . a durable possesion of daily usefulness, providing closest, cleanest, fastest shaving, it's a gift of good grooming—a constant reminder of gift-giving thoughtfulness.

A whopper of an entry (I can say that because it isn't mine), which brought its writer a whopper of a prize: Remington stock.

Can you pick out the alliteration, the Mystic Three? Notice, too, that the writer followed the sponsor's lead-in. She not only stressed all the selling points of the product but she cleverly tied them in with the purpose of the contest—to give Remington shavers as gifts. If she had failed to do that, she would have failed "appropriateness to subject."

This particular entry did not contain any eye-flagging words—no puns or plays on words—nothing but good solid sales points presented in a pretty package of appealing words. The judging agency in this case liked the plain-talk type of entry, so this knowledgeable contester gave the judges what they wanted . . . and she got what she wanted. There are other judges, however, who like some cleverness to shine through and that's where Red Mittens comes in.

WHO WEARS RED MITTENS?

Your entry should. If it could stand up, wave a red mitten and holler, "Yoo hoo, Judge, here I am! Look at me!" you'd have a pretty good chance of being noticed in that crowd of competition. Well, that, in effect, is what you can do with words. You can take some liberty with the language, play around with words, and come up with catchy ways of catching eyes, and "ayes" (that's a Red Mitten) from judges. Phrases like:

> wagging her TALES behind her
> one ASSET TEST will prove it's true
> try this on for SIGHS
> GRIME doesn't pay

These word tricks often delight a judge who has been looking at the same old stuff all day long. He's pleased to find something new and fresh in his pile of entries. So *you* want to be the one who put it there.

Caution: Do not make your entry so clever that it becomes obscure. Remember, the judge must understand it on first reading. It must be glance clear. If he's going over 100,000 entries, he's not likely to take a great deal of time to decipher your terribly clever one. Make it smart, but keep it clear.

Now that we've talked about Alliteration, Mystic Three and Red Mittens, let's see if you can put them all together in a statement. I'll give you the sponsor's lead-in and all the points covered in the winning entry. It will be up to you to eliminate unnecessary words, put what's left into one sentence (remember dashes and colons and hyphens), and still stick to the twenty-five word limit. Obviously, you won't be able to get it word for word, probably not even close, but the challenge will be interesting and the practice helpful. The actual entry will be found later on in this chapter under the heading, *Your Turn—Answers*. And don't be discouraged by your first attempts. In no time, you'll be using these devices automatically.

The sponsor was San Giorgio Spaghetti, and they asked for the completion of the following sentence: *I'd like to go to Italy because . . .*

The winning entry covered the following points:

- my sister went to Italy
- she raved when she came home
- the food was fabulous
- the views were exquisite
- she did some marvelous shopping
- I'm jealous of my sister

Hint: This entry incorporated the Red Mittens "wagging her TALES behind her."

All right, see what you can do with this information, and remember, do it in twenty-five words, or less.

YOUR TURN

I'd like to go to Italy because . . .

MORE DEVICES—
PUNS, PARODIES, PLAY ON WORDS

All of these word tricks fall under Red Mittens, and they often overlap to such a degree that you can hardly tell if you've created a pun or a parody. No matter. We don't really have to know what to call them as long as the judge calls them winners.

The previously cited "wagging her TALES behind her" is a perfect parody because the word TALES replacing TAILS in the well-known nursery rhyme has the same sound, and is a particularly apt phrase for someone talking about where he's already been. Other parodies that have appeared in winning entries are:

> a place in the FUN
> Jack of all AIDS
> Home NEAT Home
> Service with a STYLE

The list is endless, but I think these few will get you started thinking of some of your own.

Punning may be the lowest form of humor, but it rates high in some contests. Actually, there are some where the entire contest is built around the pun. Take this oldie, but goodie, from SWIFT meats. The object was to use their product names in a statement, and of course, puns would have to win. How else could you be humorous (which was one of the judging standards) about frankfurters, chili, chicken, and the like, without relying on puns. And a winner was:

> <u>Pard</u>on me for <u>bee</u>fing, but <u>frank</u>ly, when I <u>meat</u> a <u>chili chicken</u>, I take it on the <u>lamb</u> before I <u>stew</u> about her cold <u>shoulder</u>.

Every underlined word (or part of a word) was either a product name or kind of product handled by SWIFT. There are parodies *and* puns in this statement; a Parody being, for example, "chili" for "chilly," and a Pun being the whole phrase (calling an unreceptive gal a "chili chicken"). This won years ago, before Women's Lib.

A Play on Words can be almost any kind of "fooling around with the language," including puns and parodies. There was an old joke that went:

Man to runner: Are you training for a race?

Man running: No, racing for a train.

Malapropisms (I went to the hospital in an ambience) and Spoonerisms (half-warmed fish, for half-formed wish) both illustrate a play on words in one form or another.

One of my favorite puns is the old story about the bear who broke into a gift shop and stole Mr. Chan's teakwood. The strangest part of it was that the bear left footprints very much like that of a young child. Mr. Chan was heard running around looking for the bear and yelling: "Boy foot bear with teaks of Chan!"

All types of word play are most effective when used in

a familiar phrase. That way the original meaning is not obscured, and the joke is easily perceived. If you go too far afield, the humor is lost to the reader and, in contest writing especially, you don't want to lose that reader, your judge. Remember, he has no time to ponder your meaning.

Let's test your PUNmanship with the following quiz. See if you can fill in the blanks with some form of word play—puns, parodies, whatever. To help you along, I've included type of product. Again, I know it's tough but that's what we're here for. The phrases were all lifted from winning entries, and by now I'm hoping that you're beginning to think like a contester. However, if I've raised your PEEK you can see the answers at the end of the chapter. (And if you didn't catch on that PEEK is a parody for PIQUE, you're not paying attention; or I'm a rotten punster.)

YOUR TURN

Example:
1. Strawberry dessert — Berried Treasure
2. Ballpoint pen — _____ for your thoughts
3. Coffee — a real _____ me-up
4. Headache remedy — a _____ pill to swallow
5. Eyeglasses — _____ Appeal
6. Diet food — breaking the _____ barrier
7. Floor wax — Easy come, easy _____
8. Cooking oil — Distinguished _____ Cross
9. Drugstore items — Ace of _____
10. Ice cream topping — _____ Best
11. Lemonade — _____ come; _____ served

12. Liquor   When it pours,
                                     it _____

Hint: Another reminder to concentrate on well-known phrases when working on the previous list, just as you should always employ well-known phrases in your entries when relying on wordplay. If any of them were totally obscure, you would be irritated instead of entertained. That's because FAMILIARITY BREEDS . . . what? . . . CONTENT, of course. Now, it may be that you're not wholly familiar with every one included here, but you can be sure they are popular enough so that a judge will (indeed, *did*) recognize each one for its cleverness.

AND YET MORE—COINED WORDS

A coined—or minted—word is simply a word *you* create, a word not found in any dictionary (yet!) but a word that conveys something special about the subject at hand. It is frequently a combination of two or more words minted together to form that new and meaningful word. Coining words for contest entries is a smart move—one way to definitely beat duplication . . . although it's been known to happen that one creative mind creates just like another. Still, the odds are in your favor that you've made your entry unique. Of course, you have to be careful that you don't go so far out that you never come back in (in the judge's eyes). By now, you should be getting the message that no matter what device you use, the final entry must be glance clear (as I've said before) and appropriate (as I'll say again and again).

Some Coined Words:

PRODUCT	COINED WORD
Combination washer/dryer called COMBOMATIC (a coined word, itself)	COMBOMAGIC

A diamond necklace, which made the contester glow with . . .	STATUSfaction
Aluminum foil; entrant heard a . . .	WRAPsody
A brand of coffee first packed in vacuum cans, without keys to open	Key-lessly canned
Ketchup	Heinzability

And now a complete entry with a very far-out coined word which won in a statement about Lipton Iced Tea (no lead-in supplied):

Lipton Iced Tea is so ECHO-NOMINAL that when family or friends ECHO "more, more," the cost is NOM-INAL so I pour, pour!

Incidentally, I submitted this entry earlier in a KOOL-AID contest and won nothing at all. Rewritten for Lipton, it won a very nice price: $500. This is not uncommon and a good reason to keep neat records. More about that later.

Even when judged by the same agency, it is possible for a nonwinner in one contest to be a winner in another. Judging standards may be different, competition is undoubtedly not the same, and you may have even broken a rule the first time around . . . but I certainly hope not! Of course, when an entry does win, you no longer own the rights to it. The sponsor, by giving you a prize, has "bought" your entry. You may rewrite an idea for subsequent contests, but the word-for-word entry may not be used again.

Have you noticed the overlapping of Puns, Parodies, and now, Coined Words? Fortunately, it's not important that you make a serious study of the differences. What is important is that you learn to think creatively and use these Red Mittens whenever appropriate. Don't worry about what category they fall into as long as they fall into favor with the judges.

Coined Words, Puns, and the like are particularly vital in naming contests and last lines, as you will see, so learn them well for statement contests, and they will carry you through almost every other kind of contest you encounter.

AND MORE—HOT AND COLD RUNNING IDEAS

Another way to make your entry take shape and stand out is a device called Contrast. It's an interesting, yet easy way to give statements a nice touch. Contrast can also be used, like all other devices in this chapter, in most contests.

Contrast means simply going from one extreme to the other, and that's the *long and short* of it. (See?) If you've ever said that someone blows *hot* or *cold,* that life has its *ups* and *downs,* that something or other was as different as *night* and *day* . . . why, you already know a lot about Contrast. Contesting contrasting is no different except more original, of course, and many statements are enhanced by this little trick. For instance:

I would like to own an RCA Whirlpool refrigerator because . . . slim styling with big capacity gives MORE FOOD SPACE in LESS FLOOR SPACE, while dependable performance assures that nothing gets left "out of the cold."

This knowledgeable contester not only employed contrast, but she summed up her entry with a good pun. "Nothing gets left *of* the cold" is a reversal of a well-known phrase, getting left out *in* the cold. Her Pun was exceedingly appropriate for a refrigerator, and the judge thought so, too. She won a refrigerator.

This same contester used Contrast in a fifty-word statement which started out like this:

I would like to take my husband to Paris because . . . the OLD WORLD would be, for us, a whole NEW WORLD of art, music, and culture . . . (The remainder of the entry was devoted to the treasures of the Louvre, etc., but it was undoubtedly that interesting beginning that urged the judge to read on . . . and on.)

AND STILL MORE—ANALOGY

Analogy is simply using the familiar terms from one field to describe another. It's a literary device that helps you write a good MEATY entry that is not only RARE, but a CUT above the competition; if it's WELL DONE, you get the GRAVY.

That's what analogy is all about. It's a much used but still highly rewarded contest device, one that never seems to go out of style. That's probably because the choices are so varied that contester after contester can employ Analogy, and no two will use it the same way twice. Some have been overused, like mathematical analogies—the product ADDS something, SUBTRACTS something else, makes joys MULTIPLY, and nothing EQUALS it.

With so many fields to choose from, it's a good idea to leave mathematics to the professors and turn elsewhere for your *gems*, those gems that will add *sparkle* to your entry.

The following is an excellent example of an Analogy, although the Analogy itself is not very far afield from the subject: frozen vegetables. But because the product is store-bought, the idea that the contester "grows" them in her freezer, and "harvests" them, makes the Analogy work and makes the entry outstanding.

I prefer Seabrook Farms frozen vegetables because . . . with Seabrook as my "green thumb," I "grow" my vegetable-garden in my freezer for failure-free "harvestings" of healthful, fresh vegetables all year through.

Analogy is easy, can be fun, is profitable . . . so take time now to learn this technique and practice it for future use. The analogous phrases following were written expressly for this lesson. They are not from winning entries, nor are they complete statements. They are merely cited as examples so you can see what it's all about at a glance before you take Your Turn.

PRODUCT	FIELD	APPROPRIATE PHRASES
cake mix	drama	my no-TALENT baking; PRODUCES results; always a HIT; HAPPY ENDING to meals
ketchup	music	HARMONIZES with other foods; makes sauces SING; adds a NOTE of class to meat loaf
fully cooked ham	photography	a SNAP to prepare; always PICTURE-perfect; HIGHLIGHT of meals; PROOF is in the eating; CLICKS with company

An aside: if you were writing a statement and had to cut words, you could always change "meat loaf" to "hamburger" in the ketchup statement (just a reminder of how it's done).

For your exercise in writing Analogy, you might start by drawing on fields that interest you. Sports are always good; baseball, football, swimming. Business endeavors, the arts, publishing . . . as I said before, the choices are endless. Because of that, there are no Answers to this section. It's up to you to make up a product, select a field, and write down some phrases. You may stumble a bit at first, but in no time at all, you'll warm up to it and be writing analogies like a pro. Have fun.

If you've done your homework, you should have an interesting list by now, and as you can see, these phrases would add an engaging touch to your entry.

Caution: Don't overdo! You must sound sincere, and your sprinkling of cue words should flow easily and be limited to about three or four per entry. Make sure the words are flattering, and don't be so taken with your abil-

YOUR TURN

PRODUCT	FIELD	APPROPRIATE PHRASES

YOUR TURN

PRODUCT	FIELD	APPROPRIATE PHRASES

ity to write analogy and think of so many appropriate words that you get carried away.

The following entry shows how one contester combined Pun, Analogy, and Rhyme to write her winning statement:

> *I like going to RKO Theatres in summer because . . .*
> *Inside, there's no simmer in summer,*
> *Blissful patrons "go steady" clear through—*
> *While "wedding" two star-filled features*
> *Makes each weekly "bill" a "coup."*

When the entry was written, the simmer-summer was a new and fresh idea which this contester came up with. It has been overworked since and probably would not fare well today. Notice that she stayed within the twenty-five word limit, even though she wrote a rhymed statement, and she won 100 dollars.

A RHYMED STATEMENT?

Yes, you can, in many cases, write a Rhyme instead of a sentence because you are not breaking the single-sentence structure. You are merely putting your words into a rhyming pattern, using colons, dashes, etc. (no periods or end-of-sentence punctuation until poem's end, please). Be warned, however: There are some judges who go for Rhyme and others who don't. If qualifiers are scarce and you can submit only one entry, you'd better stick to a straight statement, using other devices to make your entry stand out. But if you have the luxury of multiple submissions and can write verse, by all means, give it a try. Be sure to stick to the word count, which is slightly more difficult when writing verse, but winner after winner proves it can be done. To wit:

I trade at (name of drugstore) because . . .

For finest service I can get
I go to Dankner's Pharmacy
For these "HEAL FELLOWS ARE WELL MET"—
They meet each need so "patient"-ly.

This entry is not only outstanding because it is a rhymed statement but also because of the parody of HAIL FELLOWS WELL MET and a play on words which takes an ordinary word—patiently—and turns it into an apt way of describing druggists who deal with sick people. Of course, we want the judge to see the connection immediately so we highlight it with quotation marks. It won a very nice pen and pencil set.

Before we leave rhyming in statement, I want to point out that even when you don't rhyme the whole thing, you can use what is called Inner (or internal) Rhyme. Inner Rhyme really makes an entry sing . . . and the following winner incorporates it twice to good advantage: —treat and beat; whiz and fizz:

Pabst makes it perfect because . . .'tis a real "Party Treat" with an *"Economy Beat,"* giving a *"whiz of a fizz"* that tickles the palate and adds smack to the lip.

Normally, I would not recommend using a word like 'tis, or any other poetic-license-type word—o'er, ere, ne'er, and the like—but it was necessary in this entry to keep within the word count. "It's" may have been counted as two words, which would have made this the verboten twenty-six. Of course, it's easy to justify its use this time because it won. If it didn't, I'd write up a nice piece about not using those words, with no exceptions.

As I said before, contesting is not a science, and sometimes you pays your money and takes your chances. But even that is part of the fun.

AND NOW—THAT PERSONAL TOUCH

Most entries automatically have that personal touch because, after all, *you* are writing the entry, and *you* are telling why *you* use the product. But you can go one step further by bringing in a situation that is peculiarly yours. A medical problem? Mother of twins? Traveling husband? That kind of thing. Let it show up in your statement, and your mailman might show up with a winning letter.

The Personal Touch in action:

I would like to go to Europe for 17 days because . . .
With friends living there,
My longing is clear—
Though enthused over statues and interesting
  places,
Most important, by far, are those FAR AWAY
  FACES!

The judge must have been delighted to find a fresh, new, *personal* reason why the contester wanted to go to Europe. Of course, she gave her reason in an interesting, eye-flagging way using Rhyme and Parody . . . but I'm sure that personalization made that entry outstanding.

And another:

This is what I like most about my favorite fragrance: Eight years and four youngsters later, a few poofs of its potent magic can still make me feel like MATA HARI— instead of MATER HARRIED. (Entry won perfume in sterling silver cigarette box.)

By mentioning actual numbers, the writer really drew a picture for the judge and summed it up in a very colorful way.

The ultimate in personalization (or close to it, at any rate) was my "no deodorant" entry mentioned earlier. Before you read the entry, I want to mention that I really did switch to DIAL for the reason mentioned, and maybe that honest admission scored high in sincerity. It's not the kind of thing a writer would dream up, and the judge obviously recognized that. There was no lead-in; just write a twenty-five word statement about why you liked DIAL soap. That gave me a little extra freedom to write:

When my doctor admonished "no deodorants," I panicked, until I discovered one soap that would safely, surely and thoroughly cleanse AND protect . . . I discovered Dial!

Another worthwhile feature of the DIAL entry is the slogany ending. "I DISCOVERED DIAL" has a nice ring to it. Sounds enough like a slogan almost to stand on its own.

SPEAKING OF SLOGANS

Everything you've read up to now has helped you to prepare and *start* your entry. Now you're going to learn how to *end* it.

After you've written all your sales points; after you've worked in your Red Mittens (or Mystic Three, Contrast, Analogy . . . or whatever strikes you right at the moment), it's time for you to sum up what you've been saying. Remember that old show-biz saw—leave them wanting more? Well, you're going to leave that judge wanting more, too—wanting more than anything to give you a prize.

Sloganlike endings may very well add that little extra something that sets your entry apart because no matter how straight-talking your entry is, no matter how devoid of contest devices, a good slogan ending might be all you need to raise your score. Obviously, a good ending won't carry a bad entry, but a good ending can save a fair one.

Take these statements, for example. Every one of these endings can stand on its own, and each one says a great deal in those last few words.

My favorite young fashion shoe is FOOT FLAIRS because . . . avoiding the false economy of low prices, I choose moderately-priced Foot Flairs for the superior shoemaking that means better looks, longer wear, <u>true</u> economy. (Slogan portion of entry: Foot Flairs means better looks, longer wear, true economy) Won another pair of Foot Flair shoes.

I like RED SCISSORS because . . . unlike useless premiums, truly valuable Red Scissors coupons, found only on quality products, enable me to get what I want while buying what I need. (Slogan: I get what I need while buying what I want) Won 1,000 Premium coupons.

Maxwell House coffee always tastes as good as it smells because . . . expertly produced and "key-lessly" canned to retain flavor, fragrance and freshness, Maxwell House is a richly satisfying, happily-blended "second-cup" kind of coffee. (Slogan: Maxwell House is a "second-cup" kind of coffee)

That last is loaded with devices—a Coined Word, mystic three with Alliteration, a Slogan Ending. By the way, you can test that Slogan Ending by repeating it after the product name: Maxwell House—a "second-kind" cup of coffee. Won carving set.

See how it sounds, how much like an advertisement? You will learn much more about writing slogans later on in the book, and that will help you put the beautiful finishing touch to your statements. Once again, you see the overlapping among the various kinds of contest writing.

And once again, I want to stress that knowing your product makes the difference between no prize, a small prize, and *the* prize. The contester who created the following entry knew she wasn't just writing about *a car,* she was writing about *a Datsun.* She went to her dealer, brought home brochures, read up on it, learned all about the car . . . and then she wrote:

I like the new Datsun because . . . the all-steel, full-ton, rugged little Datsun—with synchromesh transmission, dual-type carburetor—gives greater power on less fuel, greater pleasure for less money. (Didn't win the car, but the transistor radio was great.)

The "slogan" is, of course: Datsun—greater power on less fuel, greater pleasure for less money.

By now you should be getting a picture of a prize-winning statement in your mind, and soon you will be getting it down on paper.

ANATOMY OF A WINNING ENTRY

How does a first-prize winner get written? Sakrete® cement mixes was running a twenty-five-word-statement contest with a first prize of an "eighty-pound bag of silver dollars." The lead-in was: *Sakrete® is perfect for making home cement repairs because . . .*

That lead told me a great deal. I wasn't going to write about anything *but* making home repairs, and I was going to think about amateurs doing it because, after all, if you were a terrific cement worker you would not have the problems that an easy-to-use cement mix would solve.

I asked my husband why Sakrete® was different from other cements, and he said the sand was already mixed in . . . you just add water. That rang a bell in my mind. Just add water—instant cement.

So now, I had two points: amateurs and instant cement. I also read the bag and a folder I picked up at the hardware store. I discovered that Sakrete® was not only easy-to-use (I'd have to find a better way of saying that!), but it was reliable. It was—I had the phrase—"firm-holding." I also knew that my husband *always* chose Sakrete, and that made it easier to put my statement together. If he, a new homeowner (which we were then), used it, it had to be a good product for home repairs.

I had worksheets with words like all-inclusive, easily kept on hand, pesky repairs, "rue-it-yourself" (because "do-it-yourself" had just become a popular phrase) . . . and more. Phrases like one-step method of mixing; a bag of Sakrete®, a jug of water, and you; simplified procedure; all came to mind. But when I finally got down to the actual entry, I discarded the cutesy-poo stuff and opted for a heavily laden-with-sales-points entry . . . one that said what I really knew about Sakrete® (from reading) and felt about Sakrete® (from discussing it with my husband). In short, instinct told me straightforward was better than sensationally smart. I'll repeat the lead-in so you can see how naturally the entry flows from there:

Sakrete® is perfect for making home cement repairs because . . . the easily prepared, all-inclusive, one-step method of mixing, makes firm-holding Sakrete® the indispensable "instant cement" that simplifies home repairs, even for amateurs.*

Incidentally, an eighty-pound bag of silver dollars added up to $2,100. But even more important than the money was winning a *first prize.*

THE WINNER SANCTUM

Following is a sampling of winning statements and the contest devices employed. Try to pick out the devices in the entry. This will help you become familiar with the techniques, and you'll have them in mind when creating your own.

ENTRY	DEVICES
[Fill in with choice of sport] is my favorite sport because . . . [Skating] only skating enables me to be so feminine, graceful, and attractively attired while engaged in athletic competition. (Prize: first aid kit; my first winning entry)	Mystic Three (feminine, graceful, attractively attired) Alliteration (attractively attired)
I would like to own an Easy Combomatic washer/dryer because . . . the ComboMAGIC way to complete washday freedom replaces outdated "Lift 'N	Coined Word (ComboMAGIC) Coined Phrase (Lift 'N Lug) Alliteration ("Lift 'N

* *Reprinted with permission from Sakrete®.*

Lug" methods in just one safer, surer, speedier laundry operation. (Prize: a collection of LPs)

Lug" and safer, surer, speedier)

I like First National Supermarket because . . . with spacious carts designed for baby's safety, I always shop speedily, easily and comfortably for necessary essentials or mere incidentals in this modern, friendly supermarket. (Prize: television set)

Mystic Three (speedily, easily, and comfortably) Inner Rhyme (essentials and incidentals)

Why I liked the movie, "The Train": THE TRAIN, my favorite "transportation," offered Burt Lancaster's electric personality, dynamic acting ability and outstanding agility speeding along the suspense track from start to finish. (Prize: Lionel trains)

Mystic Three (electric personality, dynamic acting ability, outstanding agility) Analogy (all underlined words— transportation, electric, dynamic, etc.; are train references) Inner Rhyme (personality, ability, agility)

My favorite Bel-Air frozen food is [Green Peas] because . . . each pea stands separately firm and succulent; plump enough for addition to stews; tender enough for baby; tempting enough for toddlers . . . an EATernal family

Mystic Three (plump enough . . . , tender enough . . . , tempting enough . . .) Alliteration (tempting enough for toddlers)

favorite. (Prize: insulated picnic bag)

Coined word (EATernal)

The Bigelow carpet I like best is [Milan-Celadon Tweed] because . . . the unmistakable elegance of wool, the masculinity of tweed, effectively expresses my position and taste, adding style and sparkle to a window-less office. (Prize: Two rooms of carpeting)

Personalization (my position)
Alliteration (effectively expresses, style and sparkle)

I think of Food Fair first because . . . properly handled produce, completely stocked shelves, exceptional meat values abound there, where I easily earn the "DISTINGUISHED BUYING CROSS" for fast, thrifty, stamp-bonus shopping. (First prize: all-expense-paid week in Jamaica, including transportation, hotel, meals, rented car)

Mystic Three (properly handled produce, completely stocked shelves, exceptional meat values)
Alliteration (properly handled produce, stocked shelves, stamp-bonus shopping)
Parody ("DISTINGUISHED BUYING CROSS")
Slogan Ending (fast, thrifty, stamp-bonus shopping)

YOUR TURN—ANSWERS

PAGE 44
1. I cannot wait (3)
2. I'll give (3)

3. good-tasting (Product name) (3 or more depending on name)
4. despite (1)
5. flavor-full (2) or flavorful (1)
6. Picture-pretty (2)

Page 49

I'd like to go to Italy because . . . my sister just came home wagging her "tales" behind her—tales of fabulous food, exquisite views, marvelous shopping expeditions —and I'm just plain jealous. (Parody: wagging her "tales" behind her; Mystic Three: fabulous food, exquisite views, marvelous shopping expeditions; Alliteration: fabulous food; Personalization: I'm just plain jealous)

Page 51

1. Berried Treasure
2. Pen-ease for your thoughts
3. a real PERK-me-up
4. a BETTER pill to swallow
5. SPECS Appeal
6. breaking the POUND barrier
7. Easy come, easy GLOW
8. Distinguished FRYING Cross
9. Ace of AIDS
10. SUNDAE BEST
11. THIRST come; THIRST served
12. When it pours, it REIGNS

3

Rhyme and Rhyme Again

Now that you've learned you *may* rhyme in statement contests, you have to learn that you *must* rhyme in rhyming contests. That announcement isn't as silly as it seems on first reading. After all, if you know anything about serious poetry, you know that "prove" is often rhymed with "love," and "pain" is rhymed with "again." Read that sentence again and then forget it . . . forever. In contest rhyming, there is no room for sight rhymes (prove–love; bough–rough); near rhymes (grant–gland) and non-rhymes (blank verse). Contest rhyming is akin to light-verse rhyming, where "again" rhymes with "den" and "love" rhymes—unpleasantly—with "shove." Remember, you're not writing Spencerian sonnets and narrative poetry; you are writing jingles and limericks.

WHAT'S A JINGLE? WHAT'S A LIMERICK?

A jingle is a catch-all phrase not even mentioned in books on writing verse. It seems to have arisen from the ranks of the ad biz and is usually a singable advertising message. However, for the purpose of clarifying the two formats, we'll call a limerick a limerick (a very definite form) and everything else, from two lines on up, a jingle. You will understand the difference very quickly, but

even if you don't know what to call the finished verse, it
won't matter. Since the sponsor usually supplies the first
line, or lines, and tells you which line to rhyme, and
frequently instructs you to *Complete this limerick,* or
Finish the jingle, you'll have all the information you
need. Which will free your brain to compose your winning entry.

Because the limerick is such a set format, let's take that
up first. There are no variations to the pattern. It contains
five lines (always) with lines 1, 2, and 5 rhyming with
each other. Lines 3 and 4, indented and shorter than the
others, also rhyme with each other. The contest limerick
will usually look like this:

> *A sterling announcer named Hite*
> *Received a most terrible fright;*
> *His microphone wire*
> *Was blazing with fire*

This particular limerick was given over the air in a
local radio contest. The announcer's name was Bob Hite,
which you must know to appreciate the line, which won
the major prize of a washing machine: He became
shishka-BOB overnight!

Once again, knowledge of the product (in this case, of
the announcer) made this entry particularly on target.

You won't come across variations on this "last line to a
limerick" very often, but one such is the previously mentioned BIC lighter limerick in which only lines 1 and 2
are given. A bonanza for the serious contester because
there is so much freedom, so much opportunity to make
an entry unique. And the playfulness of the first two lines
also adds to the pleasure of working on a contest like
this.

Jingles are not as restrictive as limericks. The sponsors
may ask, as DIAL soap once did, for a couplet (two lines
only that rhyme with each other)—the uniqueness of the

DIAL couplet being the portion given. They started the couplet with *DIAL is wonderful;* the entrants had to complete that first line, and add a second. Another field day for the real contester because here, again, was a chance to shine, to really "create," to give yourself your own rhyming word. One such winner was:

> *Dial is wonderful, it is this teacher's pet;*
> *Makes me sure of my "class"—it has never*
> *failed yet.*

Notice the Analogy in that entry and the personalization. Certainly a teacher wants to feel secure about her freshness . . . and this one conveyed the feeling in some nicely chosen words. And in perfect rhyme.

The following winner used a Coined Word to make her entry stand out. Once again, the first line was not a full line, which gave her the opportunity to write her own rhyming word:

> Pineapple chunks from Dole *are a pure,*
> *perfect ending*
> *To a feast or a snack—they provide "Happy*
> *Blending."*

Sponsors may choose to give you three lines and ask for a fourth or one line and ask for a second. It really doesn't matter what the format is. What matters is what you do with it. And what really matters is meter.

METER MATTERS

Every piece of verse is made up of two equally important parts (aside from the content): Rhyme and Rhythm (or meter). Rhymes are easy. You can rhyme June and moon in your head; you can consult a good rhyming dictionary; you can use other tricks which you will learn about in this chapter. But Meter is another matter. Unless you're

Ogden Nash (and which of us is?), you cannot have a short line and a long line rhyme with each other.

Line length has nothing to do with *number* of *words*, but rather with *number* of *syllables*. While "way" *rhymes* with "okay," they're lacking in Rhythm (Meter) because "way" is one syllable and "okay," two. Easily corrected, though. We put another syllable in front of "way" to make it conform. Now, that syllable doesn't have to be part of the word itself (like halfway; out-weigh). It can be another word altogether:

> *my way*
> *okay*

Now, they work. We'll go even further and add some more syllables (in front again, because those rhyming sounds must come at the end of the line):

> *out of my way*
> *and it's okay*

Don't be confused by the fact that each phrase has four words in it; it's still the syllables we're concerned with, and we can achieve the same effect (correct meter) in a variety of ways:

> *it's not hearsay (3 words)*
> *compact bouquet (2 words)*

or even a single word with four syllables:

> *papier-mâché*

But syllables—*alone*—do not a meter make. Meter is also the combination of accented and unaccented words. In the previous examples, we could not have included holiday as one of the rhyming words because *correctly* pronounced the word is HOL–i–day. To make it rhyme with okay it would have to be pronounced hol–i–DAY

. . . and that's unnatural. Rhyming words, and all the words in your verse for that matter, must be correctly pronounced, the way they would normally be spoken.

For another example, try:

> *free;*
> *whiffletree.*

Not good, but try:

> *fancy free;*
> *whiffletree.*

Ah, that's better.

Although these two words are three syllables each, that does not mean that all three-syllable words, ending in the "EE" sound will be in correct meter. If the accents don't fall in the same pattern of accented and unaccented syllables, it won't scan (conform to metrical principles). Such a word is "energy." It's EN–er–gy . . . not en–er–GEE. This is known as forcing a rhyme and is also known as a no-no.

In the following list, some words are correctly rhymed with fancy free and whiffletree, and some are not. Can you pick the right ones out?

comedy	pedigree
chimpanzee	bumble bee
openly	tapestry
lovely	C.O.D.
absentee	master key
quality	sportily
apostrophe	disagree

I'm not going to make you wait for the answers in this case because I'm anxious to have you learn the very fine points; I really want you to accentuate the positive. *Your Turn* will come later.

By rewriting the list of words with the accented portion of the words capitalized, I hope to give you a clear understanding of meter. The correct rhymes are all accented on the final syllable:

COM-e-dy	PED-i-gree
chim-pan-ZEE	BUM-ble bee
O-pen-ly	TAP-es-try
LOVE-ly	C.O.D. (all accented)
ab-sen-TEE	MAS-ter KEY
QUAL-i-ty	SPORT-i-ly
a-POS-tro-phe	dis-a-GREE

By the way, you can find out which syllable of any word is most accented by looking it up in the dictionary. The word "comedy" would have next to it, in slash marks, its phonetic spelling which looks like this: ′kam-əd-ē or käm′-əd-ē. Without getting into details about phonetics (there's a pronunciation key up front in the dictionary which can explain it all to you), it's the stress mark that looks like this ′ which you're interested in. The heaviest emphasis goes either on the syllable before or following the stress or accent mark. Sometimes a word will appear to have two accent marks, one on top and one on bottom, as in absentee, which spelled phonetically looks like this: ˌab-sən-′te or abˌ-sen-′tē. The accent mark on the bottom means that's the second most strongly stressed syllable in the word. For our purposes right now, we're looking for the strongest syllable.

Now, all of the words just mentioned will be found together—under Ē, which means pronounced "EE"—in the rhyming dictionary. But if you're a purist about meter, you would select only words of like accents; QUALity, COMedy, SPORTily, all rhyme nicely with each other, as you will hear if you say them out loud. Actually, most *ty* and *ly* endings do not have the proper beat for the "Ē" sound, unless mispronounced. Now, it is possible that some words, apostrophe, for one, may be acceptable in a written piece of verse; and surely there

will be contest jingles where the meter is off and winners, too, for that matter, with limping meter. But you
must, as they say, learn these rules before you can break
them. In the previously cited "holiday," I would certainly not hesitate to use it at the end of my line if I had
a superior line and felt that the line flowed so well, the
judge himself would put the accent on the last syllable.
It happens, and it happens often.

There are names for and further explanations of metrical feet (as this whole business is called), but I really
don't want to complicate your life any further just now.
For contest purposes, you just have to keep practicing
and listening until you suddenly and automatically get it
right. If you're interested in learning more about meter,
a good rhyming dictionary (which you should buy) can
give you more information than you probably want. For
now, it's more important to know how to do it, not what
to call it.

However, you *must* learn that there are different ar-
rangements of accented and unaccented syllables in a
line of poetry. To put it as simply as possible, there is a
rhythmical pattern, a beat, to a line of poetry. You don't
write up a line consisting of, let's say, eight syllables,
and let the accents fall where they may. Nope, you line
them up to match each other . . . so if Line 1 has accents
falling on the second, fourth, sixth, and eighth syllable,
the rhyming line will also have accents falling on the
second, fourth, sixth, and eighth syllable. In "da–dum"
language, the line would look like this (say it out loud
and emphasize the DUMs):

da-DUM da-DUM da-DUM da-DUM

Do you hear it? Do you hear the rhythm, the beat? Here
are a set of words to go with the above "da-DUMS."
Again, say them out loud because it's essential that you
do hear the beat:

non-GREAsy FOOD's a CINCH with SPRY

Or, for something more familiar, rather than contesty:

I THINK that I shall NEVer SEE

The metrical pattern of 2–4–6–8 is quite common, but

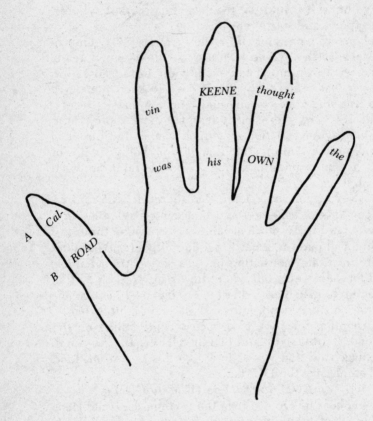

there are others frequently used in contests. Like accents falling on 3–6–9:

da-da-DUM da-da-DUM da-da-DUM

In other words: *You would THINK that big JACK would have KNOWN*

Accents falling on 2–5–8 or: *A SMART little LAdy named KAY*

Accents on 2–5–8 and 3–6–9 are always used for limericks, with the shorter lines usually running five or six syllables.

If you were writing to sell light verse instead of writing to win contests, I'd advise you to stick to the most common until you had gained enough expertise with the craft to experiment. However, the people who create contest jingles often give us lines of seven, nine, even eleven syllables, sometimes without any clear-cut rhythmical pattern, as you will see from examples later in this chapter. The line you have to rhyme, though, is often more precise, and that is always the clue to what your line should be. In any event, always recite the lines *out loud* and learn to "da-DUM da-DUM" them for yourself. An easy way to do this is to beat out the rhythm with your fingers and notice on which finger the natural accents fall. Again, if you have to mispronounce a word to make it conform to the pattern you're seeking, seek something else to say.

It's easier to count on the fingers of one hand, returning to the thumb for syllable 6. When you test the first line of a limerick using the old *drum-the-fingers-on-the-table* system, you should come out with something like this (read Line A from thumb to pinky, then go back to thumb and read Line B). The line is *Calvin Keene thought the road was his own* and the accents fall on 3–6–9: see page 76.

The second line of this limerick—That his SEAT at the WHEEL was a THRONE—is also 3–6–9, so a wise contester would surely write a line with the same meter. If lines 1 and 2 had been 3–6–9 and 2–5–8, which is often seen in limericks, line 5 would be equally correct in either meter. Sometimes, I admit, it's really a matter of what sounds right and that comes with a practiced ear. Learn to do it right, and then be flexible enough to follow your instincts, especially if those instincts seem to be working for you.

By now, you should know enough about meter to understand the following exercise. Below is the first line of a rhyme with two choices for the second: one in correct rhythm, the other limping along. Read them through; give them the "da-DUM" treatment; check the one you think sounds best:

Can't wait to enter contests now . . .

A) Because I'm really learning how
B) Because really I'm learning how

If you think the lines are identical, you haven't been paying attention. In one line the accents fall in the wrong places (on the wrong fingers); it does not conform to the given line.

Did you check A? You get an A.

Here it is again, with the accents accentuated:

Can't WAIT to ENTer CONtests NOW . . .

A) *BeCAUSE I'm REALly LEARNing HOW*
B) *BeCAUSE REALly I'm LEARNing HOW*

B, of course, suffers from a serious case of "Limping Meter." Same words, same number of syllables, same rhyming word. One important difference: one's a loser.

If you see the difference, if you hear those beats, if you understand the placement of accented and unaccented syllables, you are well on your way to writing successful (prize-winning) last lines.

THE SCENE OF THE RHYME

I've already mentioned a rhyming dictionary in passing. Now I'm going to mention it again—no, not mention—*push it*. In truth, I'm going to stop just short of insisting.

Look at it this way. If you use the obvious words, the ones that come to you as you mull over the given lines, you know those words are going to occur to the rest of the "mullers." Now, that is not to say that some of those ordinary words won't make it, or that every winner will have an unduplicated, truly sensational, rhyming word. But you do want to give yourself every advantage, and part of that advantage is having the best words to pick and choose from. If it turns out that your choice is not uncommon, it should be because you chose to use it, not because you couldn't think of anything better. A rhyming dictionary puts those choices at your fingertips and you never have to settle for the words that "come to mind."

However, here is something you can do to get started without the rhyming dictionary. It's called a "Mental Rhyming Dictionary"* and is a good, and immediate, substitute.

A MENTAL RHYMING DICTIONARY

Shortly before 1920, I invented a mental rhyming dictionary, to be used when a printed one is unavailable. Write down, having memorized them in advance, all the possible consonantal sounds in the language. Here is a convenient way:

---

* *From Clement Wood's* New World Unabridged Rhyming Dictionary *by permission of William Collins Publisher's, Inc.*

SINGLE SOUNDS	DOUBLE	TRIPLE	RARE
Vowel (no consonant)			
B	BL, BR		BW
CH			
D	DR		DW
F	FL, FR		
G	GL, GR		GW
H	HW		
J			
K (C)	KL, KR, KW (QU)		
L			
M			
N			
P	PL, PR		PW
R			
S	SK (SC), SL, SM, SN, SP, ST, SW	SKR, (SCR), SKW, (SQU), SPL, SPR, STR	SV
SH	SHR		
T	TR, TW		
th (thin)	thR		
TH (this)			
V			VL
W			
Y			
Z			ZH, ZL

This gives 23 single sounds; 24 double sounds; 5 triple sounds; and 8 rare sounds, or 60 altogether. Now apply your sound to be rhymed to this, and write out the rhymes that occur to you. Thus rhymes for *mate* would be found to include—I run down the list rapidly:

ate, abate, date, fate, gate, hate, Kate, late, pate, rate, sate, tete-a-tete, wait (single sounds); freight, great, crate, plate, prate, skate, slate, state, trait (double sounds); straight (triple sounds). None of the rare sounds.

Be careful also to add next the minor accent rhymes, of the general type of:

syndicate, conglomerate, abbreviate, indicate, intimate.

Then go ahead and use this specially prepared rhyming dictionary. The same can be done with 2-syllabled rhymes (as, for *backing*):

hacking, jacking, lacking, packing, racking, sacking, tacking; blacking, clacking, cracking, quacking, slacking, smacking, stacking, tracking.

An omitted pair are found in *thwacking* (thW) and *whacking* (HW). The same thing can be done with triple or longer rhymes.

All right, let's see how well you can apply it when writing a last line. The following limerick was one in a series of monthly contests conducted by the National Safety Council for at least twenty-five years, possibly longer. They have recently discontinued them, but contesters everywhere are hoping that a deluge of mail to the Council will get these delightful limerick contests back to us again. In the meantime you can practice up . . . just in case.

This particular limerick was directed to the "road hog." I'll count out the meter for you because there is a slight variation in line 3. You will see an extra syllable in the beginning of the line, which is acceptable as long as it is an *unaccented* syllable. Read the line out loud twice, once with the word "but," once without it. You should be able to hear the correctness of it, either way. The sense of the verse makes "but" an important word; he did this *but* then that happened.

Anyhow, you're not as concerned about lines 3 and 4
—except for content—as you are for matching the meter
of lines 1 and 2. With the aid of the Mental Rhyming
Dictionary, or with your own ideas, complete the limerick.

YOUR TURN

*Calvin **Keene** thought the **road** was his **own;***
*That his **seat** at the **wheel** was a **throne.***
*But his **kingdom** has **crumbled***
*King **Cal** is now **humbled***

_____

Make a list of rhyming words, first:

Jot down ideas about road hogs:

Write your last line here:

Do *not* look for the actual winning entry . . . *yet!*

How do you like your line? Did you really work on it, or did you settle for the first thought that came to you? Were you so anxious to get it written that you were satisfied—maybe even delighted—that the thing rhymed and the meter came out right?

If your line was something on the order of: *And he learned things that he should have known,* you just didn't dig deep; you didn't discard your weak ideas and then get going. If you were the judge and you were reading ordinary, yawnable entries all day long, would you be pleased enough with your line to surPRIZE the writer of it?

If not, read on. And if yes, read on, too. If you really did come up with something good, that is no reason to stop now . . . because *now* you want to find out what you did right so you can keep doing it, again and again. Remember, you want to be a *consistent* winner.

All right, now, go back to your worksheets and look over your lines. Anything catchy, clever? Did you include any contest devices? If not, don't give up. You get another chance before you make your final entry.

CONTEST DEVICES—AND HOW TO INCLUDE THEM

If you're going to say something special about a product and you have only seven or eight words (maybe only four or five, depending on the number of syllables in each word), you must carefully select those words. Each one must have an important place in the line and not be there just to fill up spaces in the meter. This is even more critical than a few "wasted" words in a statement. Also, you want to be unique but not far-fetched; clever, but not obscure; outstanding, but not insincere. How to accomplish all this? Red Mittens will do it; Mystic Three, definitely; Alliteration; Contrast; Analogy. Even slogan-like endings. Parodies, Puns, Play on Words. Everything! All these devices will make your last line last long—long enough to reach the senior judges. I saved Coined Words for the end because it is pure delight when you can make up an apt, important word as your rhyming word. That's one way of choosing a word that is not likely to be heavily duplicated.

Caution: Don't make up such an outrageously original word that nobody can understand what you're talking about. It's nice to be outstanding, but it's not nice to be standing out of the running because the judge can't make sense out of your "mystical minting."

Here are some examples of contest devices properly used in last lines:

THE JINGLE: *Take the smoothest vanilla ice cream;*
                     Add chocolate bits and cherries, too;
                     It's Cherry Cherie from Foremost

ONE WINNER: *Best "CANDIEDate" when PARTY's due.*
ANOTHER: *With "best fruit forward," chips to chew.*

1. Analogy (candidate, party); Pun (*candied*ate): both apt because ice cream is a party treat and this one is "candied" with chocolate bits. Nothing too obscure there.

2. Takes "best foot forward" and puns it into "best fruit forward," an apt phrase for ice cream with cherries in it. "Chips to chew" is apt and alliterative.

Another example of devices in a winning line: Analogy and Pun. First the given lines, then the winner:

> *If you want a glass cleaner delight*
> *That will keep all your windows real bright*
> *Try SPARKLE and see*
> *How pleased you will be*

WINNING LINE: *For this GLASSmate's been "schooled" to clean right.*
(Won 100 dollar gift certificate.)

And another, Mystic Three, makes up the second line of the following jingle:

GIVEN LINE: *For making toilets sparkling clean . . . use "Jonny Mop" today;*
WINNING LINE: *Hands don't touch mop, drains do not stop, no germs to go astray.*
(Won party-size coffee maker.)

Although the given line seems to be an overly long, unwieldy line it can be broken down to two lines of uneven length (perfectly acceptable):

For making toilets sparkling clean   (2–4–6–8)
Use "Jonny Mop" today   (2–4–6)

This combination of 2–4–6–8 followed by a line of 2–4–6 is a very common pattern frequently found not only in contest rhymes but in light verse as well. Make it a point to read and count out the light verse you come across in newspapers and magazines.

By breaking this down to a simplified pattern, the writer was able to come up with her lines:

Hands don't touch mop, drains do not stop   (2–4–6–8)
No germs to go astray.   (2–4–6)

Of course, when she submitted it, she wrote it out as a single line . . . and let's take another, closer look at that line. By using the Mystic Three, the writer was able to bring in three important sales points (about par for the last line course), and she concluded with a slightly unusual rhyming word and did it in a way that made it seem uncontrived. On top of all those goodies she added Inner Rhyme, which often wins.

INNER RHYME—AND WHY IT WINS

Inner or Internal Rhyme is simply a matter of making two of the accented syllables within your line rhyme with each other. They can also rhyme with the last word if you can work it out smoothly, but too often that triple rhyming can't be done without sounding forced. As you can see from the previous entry, there was nothing contrived about "Hands don't touch mop; drains do not stop," yet the lilt gave the line a nice poetic quality. (And any time you can be poetical about cleaning toilet bowls, you've made a friend out of the sponsor!)

Another example of Inner Rhyme in a last line is this bit of verse about frozen vegetables:

   Best taste; no waste—"fresh" can't outdo.

This, too, mentioned three sales points in one line.

Incidentally, this was the concluding line of a verse written for a statement contest. The lead-in was:

I prefer Seabrook Farms frozen vegetables because . . .

> *French-fries are "starched-collar" crispy;*
> *Greens "strut" in their flavorful hue;*
> *Every Seabrook sings of quality*
> *Best taste, no waste—"fresh" can't outdo.*

Notice how much was said in one little jingle and the colorful language used to add a little sparkle to the entry. Line 3, of course, has that unaccented extra beat I mentioned before. It limps a little, but not badly, because "every" is not pronounced "ev-e-ry" but "ev'ry." Even with the meter slightly off, the total effect was good enough to make it work. I admit it won only a minor prize . . . but they're nice, too.

When using Inner Rhyme always be sure that your words are well chosen.

Another one of those *Cautions:* Don't get so impressed with your ability to incorporate Inner Rhyme that you substitute a weak rhyming word for a strong descriptive word. Good Inner Rhyme means not having to sacrifice something better to use it.

ANOTHER NEW DEVICE—ACROSTICS

There is no better way to explain an acrostic than to show an acrostic.

THE CONTEST: Ten reasons why I like Frank Sinatra

THE WINNER (easy for me to write since I *love* Frank Sinatra):

> *Friendly, captivating smile*
> *Rates an "A" for singing style;*
> *Acting talent beyond compare;*
> *No role's too tough for him to snare;*
> *Kind of easy-going way;*

<u>I</u>ndependently blase;
<u>E</u>yes that twinkle merrily;

<u>B</u>oyish, charming quality;
<u>O</u>bviously, that man can soothe;
<u>Y</u>ears of show biz made him
    smoothe.

Reading down, of course, you see who the verse is about, and that's what an acrostic is about. Although it can be written in prose, it's much more effective when rhymed. An acrostic is a handy device because you can select the word or words you want to spell out, not necessarily a product name. It might be a benefit like *health, enjoyment, good taste* . . . whatever.

And if you really want to test your skills, and your sanity threshold, try a *double* acrostic with the first letters forming one word, and the last letters another.

No example. I pass.

The Winner Sanctum at the end of this chapter will give you more examples of contest devices in action, and by the time you've studied them, you should have a clear idea of what you can put into your line to make it outstanding.

But before I sum up what you can do, let's take a look at what you can't do.

INVERSIONS—AND WHY THEY SHOULD BE WRITTEN NEVER

William Shakespeare can say, "Full many a glorious morning have I seen," and Robert Frost can muse, "Whose woods these are I think I know," but they weren't writing winning contest entries. You and I have to say "I have seen full many a glorious morning" (if we happened to use words like "full many") and, "I think I know whose words these are."

Lines of verse—as opposed to lines of serious poetry

—are always written in straight conversational tones. When you worked on the limerick did you invert your words? In other words, *did you phrases write in a way that people speak not?* No good.

Whenever we find ourselves inverting words to make the rhyme come out right, we're guilty of . . . hmm! . . . inverting our words to make the rhyme come out right. Remember how those Red Mittens stood up and shouted, "Yoo hoo, Judge, look at me"? Well, inversions stand up and shout, too. They call out, "Yoo hoo, Judge, I don't know much about writing verse, but look, I make it rhyme in spite of that." One exception is when you're *deliberately* fooling around as I was when I paraphrased "one swallow does not a summer make" with my "syllables alone do not a meter make." But the play on words must be *obvious*.

So . . . if you find yourself talking backwards, *stop*, turn around, and start over. You may have to discard a good idea if you can't write it up without going into all kinds of language contortions, but discard . . . and move on.

And speaking of languages, stick pretty much to English. It is tempting, sometimes, to stick in a foreign phrase (to show off, maybe?), and I've tried it myself with well-known phrases—and without success. I don't recall ever winning with one, and all the winners I interviewed said they rarely, if ever, did. A good rule is: If you have to rely on strange words to get your point across, maybe you're working on the wrong points.

It's time for you to work again, harder than you did before. Well, I never promised you a *prose* garden. For verse, you work! Go back to your worksheets to see if there is anything worth salvaging. Maybe you *almost* had it. Maybe now that you've been reminded of old devices and learned some new ones, you'd like to try to improve on what you did before. Or perhaps you'd rather forget that and start out fresh. Either way, you now have a chance to use some of the tricks you learned in this chapter. Because what we have here is . . .

YOUR TURN TO DO BETTER

Same limerick:

> *Calvin Keene thought the road was his own*
> *That his seat at the wheel was a throne.*
> *But his kingdom has crumbled*
> *King Cal is now humbled*

Now, instead of the Mental Rhyming Dictionary, I'm giving you a page, the complete rhymes for the sound ŌN (pronounced own), from *Wood's Unabridged Rhyming Dictionary*. Here are the rhyming words the contester had for her winning entry in this contest. Right now, you are competing with her. Go to it.

ŌN

Vowel: dis-ōwn', ōwn.

b: back'-bōne, bōne, knuck'le-bōne (nuk'l-), mar'rōw-bōne, trom'bōne, whāle'bōne (hwāl').

bl: blōwn, flȳ'blōwn, fresh'-blōwn', full'-blōwn', out-blōwn', un-blōwn', weaTH'ēr-blōwn (weTH').

d: con-dōne', Dōane, Dor-dōgne' (-dōn').

dr: drōne, là-drōne', pà-drōne'.

f: an'ti-phōne, au'di-phōne, dic'-tà-phōne, ē-lec'trō-phōne, gram'à-phōne, graph'ō-phōne, meg'à-phōne, mī'crō-phōne, phōne, rā'di-ō-phōne, sax'ō-phōne, tel'ē-phōne, vīt'à-phōne, xyl'ō-phōne (zil').

fl: flōwn, hīgh'-flōwn' (hī').

g: bē-grōan', full'-grōwn', gràss'-grōwn'', grōan, grōwn, hälf'-grōwn' (häf'), moss'-grown'', ō''vēr-grōwn', un-grōwn'.

h: hōne.

j: Jōan.

k(c): Cōhn, cōne, ō-chōne'.

kr: crōne.

l: à-lōne', Ath-lōne', Böu-lōgne' (-lōn'), Cō-lōgne' (-lōn'), eau dē Cō-lōgne' (ō dē), lōan, lōne, mà-lōne'.

m: bē-mōan', mōan, mōwn, rē-mōwn', un-mōwn'.

n: fōre-knōwn′ (nōn′),
knōwn, un″bē-knōwn′,
un″fōre-knōwn′, un-
knōwn′.
p: çorn pōne, dē-pōne′,
dis-pōne′, im-pōne′*, in-
tēr-pōne′, pōne, pōst-
pōne′, prō-pōne′.
pr: prōne.
r: çha′pēr-ōne, ci′ce-rōne,
Rhōne (rōn), rōan.
s: rē-sewn′ (-sōn′), rē-
sōwn′, sewn (sōn), sōwn,
un-sewn′, un-sōwn′.
sh: fōre-shōwn′, shewn
(shōn)*, shōne, shōwn.
sk(sc): scōne.
sl: Slōan.
st: brim′stōne,
çling′stōne, çor′nēr-
stōne, çūrb′stōne,

flag′stōne, foun-dā′tion
stōne, grīnd′le-stōne*,
grīnd′stōne, hāil′stōne,
head′stōne (hed′),
heärth′stōne, hō′ly-stōne,
im-pōs′ing stōne,
kēy′stōne, līme′stōne,
lōad′stōne, lōde′stōne,
mīle′stōne, mill′stōne,
mọọn′stōne, sōap′stōne,
stōne, whet′stōne
(hwet′).
t: à-tōne′, bār′i-tōne, in-
tōne′, mac̱′rō-tōne,
mon′ō-tōne, sem′i-tōne,
tōne, un′dēr-tōne.
thr: dē-thrōne′, en-
thrōne′, ō-vēr-thrōwn′,
thrōne, thrōwn, un-
thrōne′.
z: en′zōne, zōne.

Additional rhyming words not used before:

Contest devices:

Your new line: _____
(The actual winner will be found at chapter's end. Won't
it be terrific if yours is better!)

* *From Clement Wood's* New World Unabridged Rhyming Dictionary
by permission of William Collins Publisher's, Inc.

ANATOMY OF A WINNING ENTRY

Good grooming aids are now a must;
And COLGATE is the name to trust;
For sparkling teeth and skin and hair

There they are, the given lines of a jingle about Colgate products. A little different because it does not specify a particular product, but it's a nice, easy jingle, nothing tricky, a good solid 2–4–6–8 all the way through. The points covered are "good grooming, trust, teeth, skin, hair." Reread the lines and you will see that you can't say anything about any *one* Colgate product because it would lack follow-through. A line like: *For sparkling teeth and skin and hair* can hardly be followed by a line talking about . . . let's say . . . toothpaste, exclusively.

So, you study the given lines to see what it is exactly that you must do to keep in step with it. In this case, I knew I had to write about Colgate products as a whole. My work sheet was filled with all sorts of general terms, and I had a few entries, not terrific. Lines like: *These toiletries will toil for fair.* I didn't like that much, but I sent it in.

Use Colgate for that SAVOIR-FLAIR. I liked this one, but as I've already pointed out, I never won with a foreign phrase. And this line kept my record straight:

They're pure! You're sure you're debonair. Nice line; Inner Rhyme; unusual rhyming word.

These aids GUARD ALL from disrepair. Reaching a bit. Using "disrepair" in connection with good—or bad —grooming was kind of farfetched. Besides, it gave the line a negative feeling, even if Colgate did have GUARDOL in it, and even if I was playing around with words.

They're MAID for MEN and LADIES FAIR. I'm ashamed to give you this one. LADIES FAIR is—what? —right, an inversion. The whole line was a feeble attempt to bring in the men's toiletries and what a great AID they are. When you look back at lines like this, you're glad they don't give demerits.

Okay. I was still missing that touch of specialness that would make my line stand out. And then I toyed around with the entire meaning . . . use COLGATE for all these needs. Stop going from brand to brand and label to label jumped into my head. Something clicked. A familiar phrase: *table-hopping*. A phrase with a rather unpleasant connotation—someone kind of flighty, flitting from table to table. A flighty consumer flitting from label to label would be: *label-hopping*. Of course! It also had an unsavory connotation. Now I knew my line would start *stop label-hopping*. I liked it. Stop label-hopping. That really said something. I had a mere three syllables to finish the thought so I summed up why you should stop label-hopping . . . because nothing was as good as Colgate . . . nothing compared to it. And there it was, the winning line. I'm repeating the jingle so you can see how the line flowed from the rest and didn't seem tacked on, a very important factor in last lines:

> *Good grooming aids are now a must*
> *And COLGATE is the name to trust;*
> *For sparkling teeth and skin and hair*
> *Stop LABEL-HOPPING—none compare!*

PRIZE: Transistor Television

THE WINNER SANCTUM

Once again, a sampling of winning entries. This time you will find winners in all types of rhyming contests, plus rhymed entries which won in statement contests. If you'd like to test yourself as you go along, cover the right side of the page and see how well you can pick out the contest devices.

ENTRY	DEVICES

GIVEN:
For shinier, easier-to-manage hair
Try Hollywood's favorite beauty
  care;
It's famous LUSTRE-CREME
  Shampoo

WINNING LINE:
One ASSET TEST will prove it's
  true.

Parody: asset test for acid test (strong enough to carry the line because it's so complimentary)

(**PRIZE**: washer/dryer)

GIVEN:
When I want to have a party,
And to entertain with flair,
I count on Stouffer's Frozen Foods

WINNING LINE:
Picnic-quick—a GALAffair.

Inner Rhyme: Picnic quick; Coined Rhyming Word minted from GALA-AFFAIR

(**PRIZE**: supply of frozen foods)

LIMERICK—4 LINES GIVEN for
National Safety Council slogan:
You would think that Big Jack
  would have known
That some jobs can't be done all
  alone.
    Too bad that Big Jack
    Overjudged his big back

WINNING LINE:
*So enlist "Tote 'em pals"—or
    postpone!*

Pun ("Tote 'em
pals" for totem
poles) plus good
solid safety
advice

(PRIZE: $5.00)

STATEMENT—My favorite grocery
store is (Waldbaum's) because:

WINNING STATEMENT:
*"Spaciousness" is keynote,
    "specials" the key
Excelling in products of prime-
    quality
Small-town assistance—big town
    decor
Makes shopping in WALDBAUM'S
    my FAVORITE chore.*

Rhymed
statement is the
only real device;
but count those
sales points!

(PRIZE: a shopping spree)

3 LINES GIVEN:
*Dogs are funny, that's easy to see
Whether mixed-up mutt or
    pedigree
But when CHOW TIME comes,
    they're sure to be*

WINNING LINE:
*Aware of Chow fare so
    YEARNestly.*

Inner Rhyme:
aware and fare;
Coined Rhyming
Word:
YEARNestly

(PRIZE: Dog Dish)

3 LONG LINES GIVEN:
*A St. Joseph Calendar on your wall
Will help your family—one and all,
It's the most popular calendar in
    the nation*

WINNING LINE:
*This "KING OF CHARTS" is "ACE
OF AIDS" in every situation.*

Pun and Analogy:
Whole statement
uses card-playing
terms. Both
"King of Charts"
and "Ace of
Aides" are puns.

(PRIZE: $5.00)

STATEMENT—Every home
medicine cabinet should contain
(St. Joseph Aspirin)

*Though wonder drugs may fill the
   bill
When someone is extremely ill;
When minor aches and pains
   aggrieve us
St. Joseph Aspirin will relieve us.*

Except for a
rhymed
statement, no real
devices.
Interesting
rhyme—aggrieve
us/relieve us.
Also does not
claim too much
for product

(PRIZE: $10.00)

I specifically included this last piece of verse to show
that not all winners are overly clever. Sometimes a simple (but good!) statement (poetry or prose) will take the
prize over a convoluted, clever entry. The above must
have been a different, and unduplicated, thought . . . and
of course, it was a rhyme in a statement contest.

YOUR TURN—ANSWERS

Winning line to "road hog" limerick on page 90:
EAGER WEAVERS are soon overthrown. Note play on
EAGER BEAVERS and how well EAGER WEAVERS
applies to road hogs; good rhyming word.
   Do you like your line better? Try to analyze why.

4
Sing a Song of Slogans

Advertisers know that a good slogan is like a bridge of words from company name to consumer's brain. If a slogan is everything it should be—if it's short, clever, catchy, to the point—it will sing out about a product and, with just a few words, remind consumers about that product. Pass a Burger King and you know you can, "Have it your way." Hear about the "friendly skies" and you know they belong to United Airlines. Even after a company discontinues a particular slogan, it can somehow remain theirs. Although Clairol hasn't used "Only her hairdresser knows for sure" for some time now, a comic can still get a laugh with the lines.

There is something special about slogans. Good ones make an impact on the public and sell products. And good ones make an impact on the judges and win prizes.

THE IMPACT-ED WISDOM TRUTH

The truth is, if you want to make that impact on the judges, there is wisdom in watching commercials. Start paying attention to them (grab your snack during the program!), and learn to pick out the slogans. They are usually the words spoken or sung at the end of the message, either right before or immediately after the product name. Like: "AMERICAN EXPRESS: Don't leave home without it." The situations in the dramatized commercials change, but "Don't leave home without it" is there at the close of every commercial. A good slogan.

When it comes to magazine and newspaper ads, skimming is out. Slogan-hunting is in. Notice that advertisers change their headlines from one campaign to another, but their slogans remain their . . . well . . . slogans. They, too, come at the end of the message, in this situation, printed at the bottom of the page before, after or under the product name.

Every ad and every commercial is a valuable lesson, because advertising slogans are no different from contest slogans. Both kinds are short, snappy and do a big job in a small space. You will often be required to write your contest slogan in fifteen words, sometimes ten, even six or seven. It doesn't matter what the limit is. What does matter is remembering that slogans, like statements or last lines, are not merely a string of words. They are planned, purposeful, well thought-out words brought together to convey a special feeling. And there are tricks to this particular trade, too.

Are you beginning to see how contest writing overlaps from one type of technique to another, from one kind of competition to another? Master one, you've mastered them all. Fair warning: There *are* some people who are better at statements—or slogans—or last lines. Don't despair if you can't seem to "get" something. Just concentrate on the area in which you excel . . . and take your prizes from whence they come.

When you start analyzing slogans, you will once again meet Red Mittens; Mystic Three, Alliteration, Parody, Pun, Contrast, Rhyme, Rhythm . . . and the rest. In addition, you will be introduced to Personification, which is simply giving inanimate objects human characteristics. For example, when I said, in a previously cited winning entry, that greens "strut," I was employing personification. I gave a green bean the power to act like a person. Another new device, Reversal, is prevalent in slogans.

Johnson & Johnson used it: "I AM STUCK ON BAND-AIDS 'CAUSE BAND-AID'S STUCK ON ME."

Using my own method of reading the ads, I recently came across some marvelous examples of word play. One such was an ad for LEVOLOR blinds. There at the end of the message (the bottom of the ad) was the line: "*Levolor—Our love is blinds.*" And my love is examples like that.

Okay, now we're going to test your S.Q. (slogan quotient, what else?). It's *Your Turn* to see if you have a good memory for slogans, or a rotten memory for slogans. The results won't mean a thing when it comes to creating your own, but a low score might push you into paying more attention to ads and commercials. In any event, the answers will vividly illustrate how slogans are constructed, so be sure to fill in the blanks, either because you know the answers or because you've checked at chapter's end. You will begin to recognize a certain quality, a lilt, a flow, a memorable sense of phrasing. I've supplied the type of product but not the name because in some cases the name is part of the slogan. I've given you half a slogan because . . . half a slogan is better than none. And I've included the contest devices, where applicable, both as an aid and as a lesson. You'll find the answers at the end of the chapter.

So . . . Right now, write now!

YOUR TURN

PRODUCT	SLOGAN	DEVICE
1. Airline	We fly the world __ ___ ___ ___ ___ ___ ___.	Reversal
2. Cigarette	Us _____ smokers would rather _____ than _____ (watch it; it's tricky).	Rhyme

3. Margarine	The ____ says ____.	Personification
4. Toothpaste	Put your _____ where you _____ ____.	Alliteration
5. Hair color	You're too young __ ____ ____.	Contrast
6. Television	The ____ goes ____ before the ____ goes ____.	Contrast; Balance
7. Scotch	The _____ Principle.	Alliteration; Parody
8. Automobile	We are _____.	Pun
9. Mayonnaise	Bring out the ____ and ____ ____ the ____.	Repetition Alliteration
10. Paper towels	The _____ Picker ____.	Inner Rhyme
11. Baby food	Babies are ____ _____.	Alliteration
12. Telephone	____ out, ____ out and ____ someone.	Repetition

You must have noticed by now that every slogan has a certain balance to it, although I made a point of it only in number 6. It is that balance that you will see again and again in slogans, even those that do not actually contain a specific contest device. Since this kind of "balanced phrasing" and/or unique viewpoint will also win in slogan contests, please continue the test. No hints, no help, no devices—just good slogans.

PRODUCT	SLOGAN	
13. Children's clothing	If they could just ____ ____ till _____ _____ _____ out.	

14. Airline   We _____ our _____ ever _____.

15. Fast food   You _____ a _____today.

16. Dish-   Softens hands while _____do _____.
    washing
    liquid

17. Cake &   Something _____ always _____ of it.
    roll mix

18. Cola drink   _____ adds _____.

19. Bank   It's _____ the way you _____ it to
                  _____.

20. Cheese   America _____ cheese _____.

21. Airline   _____ is _____ when you are.

Slogan contests seem to occur in phases (or phrases?). They're around for a while, they disappear, they come back. When you do come across a slogan contest, work at it. Apply all the advice and winning help given for statements and rhymes. If there is one pitfall in slogan-writing, it's the, "Oh, it seems so easy," one. Toss out your first ideas, as usual, because if they came to you that quickly, you know what? Right, you're not alone.

Now that I've pounded that thought into your head, I have to make an exception. There are times when the obvious *does* win, and there is no way I can look over your shoulder and give you the thumbs-up-and-thumbs-down routine. I can't do it for myself! It is sometimes impossible to judge all your own material because you don't know what the competition is.

All this is a build-up to the *Anatomy of a Winning Entry*, which breaks a lot of rules.

ANATOMY OF A WINNING ENTRY
OR HOW COME IT WON?

The Long Island Rail Road had special trains going to the World's Fair in Flushing, Long Island (New York).

They sponsored a contest asking for a slogan that would remind people there were trains to the Fair. One of the winners was selected from this group of six, all submitted by the same contester. Can you pick it?

> "We FAIR thee well"
> WE'LL RACE YOU TO THE FAIR
> First and FAIRmost
> WORLD BEATER to the WORLD'S FAIR
> GET ON THE RIGHT TRACK
> We "make tracks" to the Fair

The first two are my favorites. "We FAIR thee well" is an excellent parody and in its tricky way assures you that the railroad will do a good job of getting you to the fair. I also like WE'LL RACE YOU TO THE FAIR because it's a perfect pun—a familiar phrase combined with the no-nonsense fact that the railroad will get you to the fair fast, even indicating they can do it better than a car can.

They didn't win.

First and FAIRmost is almost *too* contesty, too much word play without enough substance. Doesn't bring in the train at all; doesn't even imply how you'll get to the fair. Might be a good slogan for the fair itself but not for the railroad.

It didn't win.

WORLD BEATER to the WORLD'S FAIR is much better. It calls the railroad a world beater (by implication), contains good repetition and good balance, a really nice slogan.

But . . . perhaps it was duplicated?

On first reading GET ON THE RIGHT TRACK looks like a winner, but think about it. It says nothing about the fair *or* the railroad and could have been a slogan for *anything*.

No surprise to anyone; it, too, didn't win.

If you've been counting, you know that We *"make tracks" to the Fair* was the winner. The line says everything it should. It indicates that the Long Island Rail

Road has tracks going to the fair, "making tracks" means to hurry, and it's short and has a nice flow.

Why were we all surprised when it won? We thought it was sure to be duplicated, that's why. Is it possible that there were others who thought of it and then discarded it because it just didn't seem unique enough?

We'll never know. But what we do know is that there are times we outwit ourselves—times we get too clever for our own good.

So if you have an excellent slogan, which this surely was, and you have enough qualifiers, as that contester did, don't discard some of your simple but good ideas.

All of which proves, once again, that contesting is not a science.

So—sometimes—when in doubt, send it out!

ANATOMY OF A WINNING ENTRY
OR THIS ONE COULDN'T LOSE

PANTASOTE PREMIUM PLASTIC ran a contest for a slogan: seven word maximum, and the slogan had to contain the product name. Since that immediately used up three words, it may be said that entrants had four words to work with. A tough assignment. It took many hours of hard work, but this contester emerged victorious . . . with a first prize trip to Rome! Here's what did it:

PROTECTION, PERFECTION, PRESTIGE

DEMAND

PANTASOTE PREMIUM PLASTIC

The winner sent me the following note:

"I personally think it won for these reasons:

1. Slogan ended with name rather than began with it (and most probably began with name).

2. The alliteration was relieved by the forceful word "DEMAND."

3. The entry had two equally good interpretations:
—these qualities require using the product

—the buyer should demand the product for these qualities."

And may I add, WELL DONE!

THE WINNER SANCTUM

I think you've had enough of slogans for the moment, so
I'll just give you a few contest winners to show how
adlike they are. I'll omit devices because by now you
should be picking them out for yourself.

Slogan for a local television station:
The FIRST word in news; the LAST word in entertain-
ment.
(PRIZE: winner did not reveal)

For one of the cancer funds:
The most you can give is the least you can do.
(PRIZE: winner did not reveal)

For a General Mills cereal of your choice:
When "sweetness counts," Cocoa Puffs score.
(PRIZE: tricycle)

To promote water safety:
Learn safety rules when you embark; make every boat
a "KNOWER'S ARK."
(PRIZE: weekend of deepsea fishing for my party of eight)

For San Antonio (contester included name in the slo-
gan):
San Antonio—where SCENIC yesterday meets
SONIC tomorrow.
(PRIZE: $50)

The following were not technically slogans; they were
written for the short-short statements (ten or fifteen
words) you will sometimes come across in your contest-

ing career. These short statements often come out sounding like slogans, as well they should to be effective, so I'm including them here.

A two-line limit on entry blank with a lead-in: *My favorite grocery store is [Bohack's] because* . . .
. . .from one item to a cartful, the service is fast, the value unsurpassed
(PRIZE: a 15-minute shopping spree in the store I chose to write about . . . what fun!)

A ten-words-or-less statement with lead-in: *I use HOTEL BAR WHIPSTIX because:*
At the end of the WHIRL . . . a better butter
    or
There's a WHIRL of a difference in WHIPSTIX
(PRIZE: perfume)

There's a very good reason why I included these two even though I don't know which entry won, rather, *especially* because I don't know. This is an example of what happens when you don't key. There's a lesson here.

Same contest; smarter contester; she keyed:
ComPATably "breadable" this spreadable edible has more pats per pound.

YOUR TURN—ANSWERS

1. We fly the world the way the world wants to fly (Pan Am).
2. Us Tareyton smokers would rather light than fight (and if you said "would rather fight than switch" you haven't been paying attention to the ads).
3. The flavor says butter (Parkay Margarine).
4. Put your money where your mouth is (Close-up).
5. You're too young to look old (Loving Care).

6. The quality goes in before the name goes on (Zenith).

7. The Pleasure Principle (J & B Scotch).

8. We are driven (Datsun).

9. Bring out the Hellmann's and bring out the best.

10. The Quicker Picker Upper (Bounty).

11. Babies are our business (Gerber's).

12. Reach out, reach out and touch someone (Bell Telephone).

13. If they could just stay little till their Carter's wear out.

14. We earn our wings every day (Eastern).

15. You deserve a break today (McDonald's).

16. Softens hands while you do dishes (Palmolive).

17. Something good always comes of it (Bisquick).

18. Coke adds life.

19. It's banking the way you want it to be (Manufacturer's Hanover).

20. America spells cheese K-R-A-F-T.

21. Delta is ready when you are.

5

Picture This

Picture yourself submitting an entry in a picture-titling contest and winning top prize. Now picture yourself reading the letter of congratulations, and let's write a title for this picture we've imagined. An appropriate title might be: "I HAVE A WIN SOME PERSONALITY." But let's take it one step further. Another contester wrote the entry, won the prize, read the letter . . . and fainted dead away. Now we have an added dimension: a picture of a contester, winning letter in hand, sprawled out on the floor. "I HAVE A WIN SOME PERSONALITY" is no longer apt; the fallen figure can't be speaking, for one, and for another, the "faint," having become a major part of the picture, should not be ignored. A title for this new picture might be "A WIN FALL." It's a parody of a well-known word, *windfall*. It's certainly apt; it has a humorous twist, and a good title. Notice that the picture has been given a title that is strictly a title. It is not a caption.

TITLES AND CAPTIONS—WHAT'S THE DIFFERENCE?

The distinction was not easy to come by. Webster's Unabridged (Second Edition) defines caption as "a title or subtitle, as of a picture." Under "title" in the same book

I have a win some personality.

A Win Fall.

Jahnus Vizon

we find "the name of a poem, essay, chapter, book picture." Four other dictionaries (including another unabridged) agreed, and so it seemed that *caption and title* were interchangeable. I had a "gut" feeling that hollered, NO. There had to be a difference since a title was merely a name while a caption could convey much more. I pursued it and, sure enough, the presidents of three major judging agencies disagreed with the dictionaries. The words were clearly not first cousins, just distant cousins. If you sent a caption when a title was called for . . . oh, oh! They all said, of course, that the rules clearly state what is wanted, and usually an example is given. *Wise move:* Follow the example.

I finally found what I was looking for, because it bothered me that dictionaries and the judges, to say nothing of my gut, were at odds. But Webster's Third had amended the definition, and under caption it says, "an explanatory comment or designation accompanying a pictorial illustration."

To carry out these definitions one step further, let's say that "Mona Lisa" is a title (the name of the painting), but if it said, "Picture of a woman who just learned the difference between title and caption," *that* would be a caption.

Many contests will call for titles *or* captions, and the rules will say, "Write a title or caption . . ." In that case, it's safe to do either. But if the rules call for one *or* the other ("Write a title for this picture," or "Write a caption for that . . ."), make sure you send the right one. Give 'em what they want, and be sure to mind your T's and C's.

T'S AND C'S AND HOW TO GET STARTED

First, you study the picture. A real study, I mean. Don't glance at it and think you've done your homework. You haven't. What you are looking for is something in that picture that others might miss. Let that picture "talk" to you. It can be the look in a character's eye that gives you the message, or a hand held in a certain way, a leg crossed, lips pursed, hat tilted. Perhaps it's the scenery —a lampost with a number, a street name, a car with a flat tire, whatever. The point is, look for the fine points.

Go *into* the picture. Go beyond what you see. Put in what the artist left out. Conjure up what has already happened. Anticipate what's about to happen. If a boy is batting a ball toward a house, you can project; you can tell where the ball will land—through a window, let's say—and call the picture GLASS DISMISSED (title). If it's a fisherman pulling up an obviously heavy catch, but no fish is showing, *you* can decide what's going on . . . and coming up. The man's expression will help create the line. Maybe he's saying: "I always get a *BOOT* out of fishing" (caption).

Caution: Don't go so far beyond the obvious that only you know what you're talking about. Remember, make it glance clear! Make sure the judge sees what you see, and your line should *clearly* point it out.

After you've made your study and after you've decided what happened or will happen, you're ready to start writing those lines.

Good advice: Keep those lines short, apt and humorous.

HOW ABOUT SHORT, APT AND SERIOUS?

In most cases, humor rates high. It is more often the cute, whimsical, playful kind of humor that wins rather than the heavy-handed, knee-slapping variety. Of course, the cartoon-type picture calling for a cartoon caption should evoke the boldly humorous line. Sponsors, even when the product is involved in the picture, are looking for the light touch, or they would run some other kind of competition.

So keep your lines light, and playful, and apply winning devices, of course.

OF COURSE! BUT HOW?

Here's how. Picture to be captioned showed a family indulging in various sports, including badminton, baseball, sailing and basketball. The following entries won small prizes:

Everyone benefits from a PLACE IN THE FUN. (parody)

Reducing the GIRTH OF A NATION. (parody)

Picture of woman about to write an entry about tobacco, and she is chewing the tobacco:

The "KNOWLEDGE GRADUATE" who believes in SELF edCHEWcation. (Pun).

Picture of Benjamin Franklin with the kite in the storm:
The cloud has a silver LIGHTNING. (pun)

Picture of the onetime Secretary of Agriculture Earl Butz making a mushroom omelet while L. A. Wilhelm, President of the American Egg Board looks on. The key here was the expressions on both men's faces as the egg was being slipped from pan to plate . . . and appeared a bit messy:
"Don't blame yourself. If there hadn't been a power failure right in the middle of Julia Child . . ." (No devices; just humor)

The following, although not technically a picture-captioning contest, is included here because you would treat it as such when working on it. It was a contest to tell what the talking KOOL-AID pitcher was saying, and the fact that it was supposed to be a "talking pitcher" did not

change the outcome too much. The contester who wrote
this did a nice job:

"For a fruity refresher, I'm at your <u>beck and KOOL</u>"
(parody; alliteration).

If the alliteration eludes you, it's the sound of "fruity
refresher." And, of course, the parody is a nicely appropriate switch of "beck and call." This entry is almost
sloganlike, and the similarity between slogans and captions can be observed from time to time in winning entries. It's the brevity, the snappiness, the saying-a-lot-in-
a-single-line that brings the two of these together.

Here's an example that comes from a purely contester's
contest. It was at a contester's convention (of which,
more later). Meetings were over, dinner was over and a
bunch of us were sitting around the convention room
making up on-the-spot contests for the others to enter.
Someone pointed to a huge picture of the signing of the
Declaration of Independence and asked for a caption. I
looked at the picture and took in all the important points.
The men in the picture sat or stood around a long confer-
ence table; one held the document in his hand while
another man stood looking down. I decided the document would be—what else?—a contest entry, and the
man studying it would be speaking. The line that *had* to
win in a group of contesters was:

"No good. She didn't hand-print her entry."

By now you should have a good idea of what captioning is all about. Remember, you can always rely on the
good old standbys: Puns and Parodies (very big in captions, as you may have noticed), Alliteration, Analogy,
Word Play, and the rest. Any Red Mittens that will make
your entry stand out will help in these one-liners. And
any advice you absorbed about slogans goes for picture-
captioning, too. With the obvious and *loud* addition of
study that picture and make your title or caption apt!

If you're wondering why I haven't put any emphasis
on titles, wonder no more. There is a good reason: Titling
(exclusively) of pictures is not too popular. Captioning

usually gets the play. However titles do win, sometimes, in the "either/or" kind of contest, such as the previously mentioned Ben Franklin with kite. Most of the winners were, indeed, captions, but some titles won, two of which were:

"Sputterfingers" (parody);

"A CURRENT EVENT" (word play).

My own personal feeling is, given the choice of title or caption, you can write either, but you can write more with a caption.

And now it's time to test your "caption capabilities." Wouldn't it be great if we had a real contest, just as it appeared in a magazine, for you to work on? Well, I just happen to have . . . well, actually, I created this contest for *Games* magazine, not knowing it would be handy right about now. So instead of *The Winner Sanctum* in this chapter, I will combine a few features, including *Your Turn.*

Sharpen your pencils, and let's get to work. . . .

THE WINNER SANCTUM
PLUS YOUR TURN—MY TURN
TO EXPLAIN MY JUDGING, AND WINNERS

I'm not going to tell you anything at all about the contest before you begin. Let's set the mood. You are reading *Games* magazine, worked a few crossword puzzles, played some word games, filled in the blanks with answers to quizzes, maybe did a cryptogram or two, and then . . . you came across this contest. All right, see what you can do. Actual winners will follow.

A FLAG ON THE PLAY

CREATIVITY, COMPETITION

Clint Miller, photographed by Ken Robbins

Grand Prize: Two season passes to the home games of the football team of your choice.

Four Individual Prizes: A GAMES T-shirt.

With the toss of a handkerchief and a small repertoire of studied poses, a fearless little man in a striped shirt lays down the law to twenty-two shoving, grunting, careening hulks of "humanity." He keeps them in straight lines, tells them when to stop mauling each other and get up out of the mud, and even makes sure they are properly attired.

We've often wondered how he manages to do it, season after season. What lofty thoughts pass through his unflinching mind? The four poses in the top row are accompanied by the comments we imagined coming through his gritted teeth at the time the photographs were taken. The four uncaptioned pictures provide the challenge of the contest.

Try your hand at creating zanily appropriate captions for any or all of the illustrations in the bottom row. An individual prize will be awarded for each pose, and a grand prize for the best single caption of all. Our favorite submissions and the names of winners will appear in a future issue of GAMES. Each caption must be 25 words or less. □

Reprinted from Games *magazine. Copyright © 1978 by Games Publications, Inc.*

WORKSHEET FOR "A FLAG ON THE PLAY"

A.

B.

C.

D.

Enter your "winning" captions here:

A. _____

B. _____

C. _____

D._____

Look them over. Are you satisfied with them? Do you think they are unique enough to be original, or do you have a sinking feeling that your line will be heavily duplicated?

MY TURN: Judging this contest was fun; there were many excellent lines and a lot of laughs. Plus a lot of

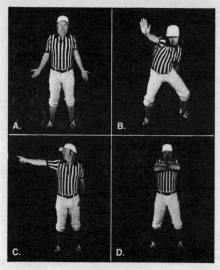

Reprinted from Games *magazine. Copyright* © *1978 by Games Publications, Inc.*

A FLAG ON THE PLAY

A wave of the yellow handkerchief to the more than 4,000 of you who sent in "zanily appropriate" captions for the poses reproduced above (July/August, page 21). Generally speaking, the most often repeated references were to pantyhose, fifth down, Howard Cosell, O.J.'s yardage gained at airports, the Goodyear blimp, and tackling, making passes at, or huddling with the cheerleaders.

The Grand Prize winner comes from the Picture A category: "He says it's his first touchdown and he'll finish his dance when he's good and ready." The contributor, Richard Evers of Parsippany, NJ, will receive two season's passes to the New York Giants.

Runners-up, who will receive GAMES T-Shirts, were:
Picture A: "I had to call something when the whistle blew. How was I to know the train comes by this time of night!" Elizabeth A. McDuff, Little Rock, AR.
Picture B: "Stop already, O.J., you crossed the goal line thirty yards back!" Al Russo, Sacramento, CA.
Picture C: "The trombones are not in line with the tuba and drums." Sarah A. Riley, Baltimore, MD.
Picture D: "I don't care what Smith said about E. F. Hutton! Get on with the game!" Bryan Martin, Micro, NC.

Other notable ideas, many ruled out for duplication, included: Referee A: didn't see what happened; thought they were playing baseball, basketball, or soccer; couldn't tell a 250 pound linebacker anything; didn't know the penalties for eating pizza in the huddle, spiking the opposing coach, or kicking the opponent through the uprights.

Referee B: had an itch, starch in his shorts, and the flag sewn into his pocket; dropped the coin; wants his wallet back; can show John Travolta a thing or two; and knows what a "split end" is.

Referee C: is tired of using his arm for the measuring stick; is drying his nail polish; is pointing to his wife, girl friend, or mother in the stands; is telling players they are going the wrong way.

Referee D: often swallowed his whistle, flag, and football; played Simon Says; will hold his breath until he turns blue, purple, sets a world record, or gets the football back; does Russian dances; is an Indian Chief; and will get the guy who tied/glued his arms.

Congratulations, winners. And a rousing cheer to all the rest who made this contest so much fun to judge.

surprises. I knew duplication would be a problem, but I didn't know *how* duplicated the ideas would be. I mean, actual word-for-word, to the point that I thought I was rereading an entry. I would have expected there would be many, "If you think I'm going to tell a linebacker what to do, you're crazy." What I didn't expect was the line, repeated even to the size and weight of the linebacker, coming from Canada, Alaska, New Mexico, California, New York and any state you can think of. I read over and over again, "If you think I'm going to tell a 6-foot 2, 297 pound linebacker what to do, you're crazy."

As you will see from the results of the contest, others were equally duplicated. I'm sure many entrants wondered why their excellent lines didn't win. Now they know.

On pages 118–119 are the contest results, just as written up in *Games*.

ANATOMY OF THREE ENTRIES—BIG PRIZE, SMALL PRIZE, NO PRIZE

The contest called for a caption in fifteen words or less. The picture showed a happy baby sitting on something (possibly a fluffy towel), and the sponsor was STA-PUF, a fabric softener.

1. "Mommy says economical Sta-Puf 'travels far,' BRINGS BACK like-new softness to wash-weary fabrics."
(NO PRIZE)

This entry tries too hard. It puts words in the baby's mouth that are artificial and lacks a kind of cuteness this kind of picture should evoke. Interestingly enough, the same contester submitted two other lines that started "Mommy says . . ." and though they were good lines, they did not win. It's possible that the "Mommy says . . ." was heavily duplicated because most people would fall into that as an easy way of putting a lot of grown-up words into this kid's mouth. It didn't work.

2. *Happy babies are made of*
   A little STA-PUF, lots of love!
   (PRIZE: three pairs of stockings)

Same contester, better entry. Notice that it was strictly a caption, not dialogue, and that's always acceptable. It also does not make too big a claim for STA-PUF by making a "little" part of the happy baby while "love" got top billing, as well it should. It's unusual for a rhyme to win in a caption contest, although a short line with Inner Rhyme often rates high. But this contester handled the rhyme well. It didn't sound forced, and it didn't detract from the content of the caption.

3. "I just love to wiggle my 'feet fingers' in our fluffy, Sta-Puf'd towels."
   (BIG (2ND) PRIZE: dishwasher)

I'm glad this was my entry so I can tell you exactly how I did it and why I think it won. I did it because I have a good memory, and it won because it wasn't duplicated. No adult could make up "feet fingers." When my son, Edward, was a baby he looked down at his bare feet one day, wiggled his toes, pointed to them, and said "feet fingers." I filed it away in my brain, and out it came for the STA-PUF contest. The rest of the entry was easy. What would the baby wiggle his "feet fingers" in? A fluffy towel. What made it fluffy? What else! I used the product and knew it really did make a difference in the towels, so I played that up. Notice the alliteration, too. But most of all, notice that the baby *could* be saying these things; words like "wiggle" and "feet fingers" and even the use of STA-PUF as an adjective rather than a noun all added to the childlike quality of the line. (It's easy to be "smart" *after* the fact; if it lost, I'd probably tell you why too!)

6

The Game of the Name

The name of the game is creating a name . . . and that's what this chapter is all about.

And speaking of chapters, have you noticed they're getting shorter? That's because you're getting smarter. All I have to do is suggest a Parody, and you might be tempted to reply, That makes CENTS. Or I'll mention Alliteration and you will probably think to yourself, That's *n*othing *n*ew *n*ow.

Not only are the chapters getting shorter, the words per entry are getting fewer. We've gone from twenty-five in a statement, to seven or eight in a last line, down to four or five in a slogan and two or three in a picture title. And now, the ultimate in brevity: *one word.* Not many writers can earn $25,000 per word, but a contest writer can, if that word is the right name for a product, mascot, toy or even a baby, which was a popular kind of naming contest at one time whenever a character gave birth on a television "sitcom."

WHAT'S IN A NAME?

A rose by any other name might smell as sweet, but a hard-to-pronounce product won't sell as well. Advertisers know that a name is very important. A good one must be memorable, give an impression of quality, tell what the product is or what it does, and on top of all that, be easy to say. MR. CLEAN is a good example. Nothing tricky there, yet it imparts a feeling of confidence in the consumer. A name like SLENDER for a diet food is more than apt: it's downright enticing (she says as she stops to have one for lunch).

Check the cereal shelf in your supermarket. LIFE, TOTAL, SPECIAL K—all snappy names that may not tell much about the product, but the sound is right and the connotation is correct: *life, total, special.* These words mean something.

Other cereal names go further; they tell what the cereal is: *RICE* KRISPIES, *CORN* FLAKES, *WHEAT*ENA. Still others employ our devices of Parody, Alliteration, Inner Rhyme: ALPHABITS, CAPTAIN CRUNCH, POST TOASTIES . . . and so it goes.

Some companies take a family name and make it work for them: *It's COTT to be good* (Parody), or they make a plus out of a minus: *With a name like SMUCKERS it has to be good.* But generally, the roll-off-the-tongue type of name is most preferred: DASH, PLEDGE, DIAL, ZEST. Longer names have that same pleasing quality: MIRACLE WHIP, CRACKERJACKS (Inner Rhyme), SEVEN SEAS (Alliteration).

Name-creating lessons are all around you. All you have to do is *shop, look, and listen* to me when I tell you to study the names of the products as you pick them up in the stores (much less aggravating than looking at the prices!). Notice the contest techniques, the ones you are already familiar with and the ones you're about to meet in this chapter. You've probably been buying JELL-O for years without once thinking about its name. Jell means to take a definite form, which JELL-O certainly does. The "O" is an Add-on, a handy little device for transforming an ordinary word into a product name. A contest winner did it when she gave a cake the name of GIGGLE-O. (Don't think "O" is the only Add-on; you will meet others shortly under the title of "New De-vices.")

BUT FIRST, THE BAD NEWS

Here's that old devil—duplication. In no other contest is duplication as much of a problem as in naming. After all, it was tough to be original with twenty-five words. Now you must be unique with one or two. That's a challenge. The advice from this corner is—are you tired of hearing it?—work up a batch of ideas, throw them away, and start over. It's a temptation, especially in naming contests, to send in the first idea that comes to you. That's because you've undoubtedly thought of an absolutely apt name the moment you read the description or saw the picture of the item to be named. You're sure you can't improve on it.

There is a classic contest story which appears in the Shepherd School Contest Course about that kind of thinking. Eighteen thousand, five hundred and fifty-eight people figured they had the one perfect name when GOLD MEDAL flour ran a contest to name a silverware pattern. It was a natural, of course, so they all sent in MEDALLION. One person called it MEDALITY and won first prize of $7,500. Not a bad reward for being just a little bit different.

THERE'S GOOD NEWS, TOO

You've already learned how to make your statements, slogans, last lines and titles stand out, and much of what you learned applies to naming. Since you're now familiar with Alliteration, Puns, Parodies and Rhyming, etc., you could have easily come up with winning names like:

GLADLAGS (Parody) for a donkey
SHORT SNORTER (Alliteration; Rhyme) for a pig
CHRISTOPAW COLUMBUS (Alliteration; Pun)
  for a puppy

SUN-SPUN (Rhyme; Alliteration) for an orange

Alliteration, Parody, Puns and Rhymes also show up frequently in trade names: HAMBURGER HELPER, MANWICH, KOOL-AID, and PALL MALL, respectively. These techniques are safe bets in naming contests.

A safer, and surer, method of avoiding duplication is to go beyond the obvious, and that calls for a slew of new devices.

A SLEW OF NEW DEVICES

All of the following techniques will help you coin names (and, incidentally, help you coin words for every other type of contest). Since many of these tricks show up in trade names, I'm going to mix and match . . . which will further prove that contest names and commercial names have a great deal in common.

FONE-ET-IKS

This is not a typographical error. I deliberately spelled phonetics phonetically (the way it sounds rather than the way the dictionary spells it) to indicate how some names are born: CUT-RITE wax paper; FOTOMAT stores; DRANO; SWEL frosting; STA-PUF. These are all examples of phonetic spelling of ordinary words. A contester used the same device when naming a lion: PEEP L. EATER. "EATER" is not spelled phonetically because the contester knew enough not to overdo it, not to get so far away from the original that the final name would lose its clarity.

The use of initials is a handy little trick, and you will see it again in other winners.

TRIK SPELLING

A distant relative of Fone-et-iks is Trik Spelling. Here, names are misspelled to add a touch of the exotic to an ordinary word or phrase. Picture this: A new pudding is developed and somebody taste-testing it exclaims, "That's a mighty fine pudding you have there, son." And a name is born that will be a household word for years to come: MY-T-FINE. All right, I invented the story, but it *could* have happened that way.

Trik Spelling is a favorite when it comes to consumer products:

CUP-A-SOUP	ZIPLOC
HANDI-WRAP	FANTASTIK
QUIK	CHEEZ WHIZ
RY-KRISP	REDDI-WIP
WISK	

And a winning cake name playing the Trik: SNOWTOPT

SPLICING

Splicing is exactly what it says it is. Something is cut out of the middle of two (or more) words, and the portion that's left is spliced together, forming a brand-new word.

Caution: After you've spliced your word, it's wise to have somebody else test it if there is a chance it might be mispronounced or misunderstood. Some spliced words may be absolutely clear with no chance of the new word being mangled: ENDUST (end dust, obviously); BISQUICK (biscuit, quick); APPLEASY (apple, easy). But in words of more than two syllables, there is always the chance that emphasis will be placed on the wrong one. This might make your name meaningless, if not downright insulting.

It's possible that MANWICH (which, as a whole, is a parody) was developed from he-MAN sandWICH. And LESTOIL, of course, tells you that you will have LESS TOIL with this product. And now, a spliced winner: BUBBLINOVER, a prize name for a whale.

The "G" is one of the most dispensable letters of the alphabet when it comes to splicing . . . as if often is in speech. We've all been guilty of saying things like, "I'm comin' over," so you can see how naturally this works out when coining names.

ADD-ONS

Sometimes just adding a letter or a syllable (remember JELL-O?) to another word produces a pleasant-sounding name. Sponsors have done it: FIGURINES (actually a spliced Add-on because they dropped the "E" before adding "INES"); MALLOMARS (an interesting concoction; they spliced it by removing the W from marsh*mallow;* and transposed the first syllable, marsh minus the "h," and used most of it for an Add-on; nice total effect with alliteration).

And the winner in a dessert naming contest: LOLLI-POPULAR (also interesting because the Add-on to LOLLIPOP made a POPULAR word out of the last syllable).

Prefixes and suffixes of all types belong in this category because they are added on, before or after a word, to give it special meaning. If you know your "roots" you can create oustanding names: DERMASSAGE (DERM meaning skin, spliced with MASSAGE, and what is the sponsor telling us? Of course! This product will massage your skin.); CUTEX (may have come from CUTICLE; suffix EX is a relocation of the normal use of EX as a prefix, meaning *away from, out, beyond* . . . or to put it my own way, *get rid of* . . .).

Words like *concertina* and *croquettes* display two common contest Add-ons, *ina* and *ettes*, often used to name something that is small, petite.

ELLES is a pleasant sounding suffix not listed in two etymological dictionaries I checked! But that doesn't make it any less valuable as an aid to naming, as one company did by taking the ordinary word COTTON and giving us a nice sounding toilet tissue: COTTONELLE.

Thought for the day: Ordinary word + suffix or prefix = EXTRAORDINARY ENTRY.

We have come, once again, to Your Turn, but I give you fair warning—this time you really have work to do. If you'd rather put it off, that's all right because you should do this when you have time to do it *all*, because this work sheet will eventually become a valuable, timesaving tool when you're working on deadlines. Don't try to do it all at once. It will get tedious and you will become annoyed and ditch the whole thing. (Do I know human nature?)

Herewith, then, some prefixes and suffixes to have at your fingertips. Check an unabridged dictionary and write down the meanings.

Aw, come on, do it; you won't be sorry.

YOUR TURN

PREFIXES

aero _____	geo_____	neutra_____
all_____	gyro _____	neo_____
aristo _____	hi _____	non_____
auto _____	hydro _____	nova_____
bene_____	inter _____	omni_____
bi _____	jiffi _____	para _____
bio _____	lava _____	perma_____
carbo _____	lubri _____	poly _____
centri _____	lumi _____	porta_____
deco _____	lustro _____	presto _____
di _____	magna_____	Prima _____
duo_____	master _____	Puro _____
econo _____	maxi _____	quali_____
enduro _____	micro _____	quasi _____
ex_____	mini _____	reli _____
favo _____	mono _____	roto_____
flora _____	multi _____	sani _____

super _____ tri _____ uni _____

tele_____ tru _____ vari_____

thermo _____ twin _____

SUFFIXES

_____ a	_____ ene	_____ ique
_____ ac	_____ enne	_____ ita
_____ ade	_____ er	_____ ito
_____ ad	_____ ere	_____ ity
_____ age	_____ eria	_____ kin
_____ ago	_____ esque	_____ let
_____ all	_____ ette	_____ lo
_____ amo	_____ ex	_____ loid
_____ anné	_____ flex	_____ lux
_____ ar	_____ giene	_____ maid
_____ ate	_____ ia	_____ master
_____ athon	_____ iac	_____ manship
_____ ater	_____ ian	_____ meter
_____ ator	_____ iant	_____ more
_____ ava	_____ ice	_____ nova
_____ away	_____ ida	_____ o
_____ co	_____ ide	_____ oco
_____ craft	_____ ille	_____ ocrat
_____ dex	_____ ima	_____ oda
_____ dyne	_____ ime	_____ ola
_____ eco	_____ ina	_____ omatic
_____ een	_____ ine	_____ ome
_____ ella	_____ io	_____ omo
_____ ello	_____ ion	_____ one

_____ onne	_____ ray	_____ tan
_____ oque	_____ ran	_____ teen
_____ ora	_____ ron	_____ tone
_____ ore	_____ san	_____ tex
_____ ova	_____ seal	_____ ward
_____ ox	_____ tain	_____ well

The thing to remember is that this list is by no means complete—not even close. And every time you discover a new prefix or suffix, add it to your ever-growing collection. It will really help you in every kind of skill contest where the creating of new words is important.

MORE NEW DEVICES

Drop-offs

Removing the first, or last, letter or syllable does just what adding one does; it transforms an ordinary word into a memorable name: FAB (fabric? fabulous? . . . whatever); LUX (deluxe or luxury, for sure); REM (remedy).

This sytem knocks a lot of G's out of the runnin', and is accomplished with or without the use of an apostrophe: CHARMIN; CRACKLIN' BRAN.

A contester did it with a name for a disc jockey show (dj's name was Bill): BILL'S APOPPIN (parody of *Hellzapoppin*)

Combos

Ah, the least complicated of all devices (that should sound pretty good right about now). Simply combine two or more compatible words and you get Combos that convey what the product is, or what it does:

SOFT SCRUB
COOL WHIP

DREAM WHIP
MINUTE RICE
RAISIN BRAN
STOVE TOP STUFFING (what alliteration!)
CLING FREE

As you can see, many of these names are truly descriptive, and descriptive names do win in contests. Winner in contest to name a station in outer space: SKIPPER DIPPER.

Another contester combined two words to create a parody of a familiar phrase pertinent to space travel. I'm not sure what category this triple-device entry falls into because it also has an Add-on . . . but this seems as good a place as any to put it in: BLAST OFFice.

DOUBLE-UPS

An extremely popular form of Combos, Double-ups *really* tell what the product is *and* does . . . or, at any rate, what the consumer does with it:

SHAKE 'N BAKE	SHORT & SASSY
STIR 'N FROST	HEAD &
SPRAY 'N WASH	SHOULDERS
SPRAY 'N VAC	NICE 'N EASY
	LIGHT 'N
	LUSCIOUS

No winners *yet* in this category, but it would be a good bet in future contests because of its recent popularity.

The ultimate in "telling it like it is" seems to apply to cake mixes and frostings where cuteness, cleverness and a snappy turn of a phrase give way to plain, sensible, this-is-it kind of talk. Names like: SUPER MOIST CAKE MIX, CREAMY DE LUXE FROSTING, MOIST & EASY SNACK CAKE MIX abound. This kind of name could definitely be an asset in a recipe contest since the name should convey what the recipe is all about, although a little cleverness can be added if its not too heavy-handed.

MORE ADVICE

Keep your Play on Words timely. Don't fool around, for
instance, with a word like *beatnick* which has just about
had it. I did once and won with *treatnik*, but it was ap-
propos at the time. I would not use it now. Today I would
use *disco, liberation, meaningful relationships.* If you
delve into the past for your ideas, they must be classic,
not faddish, phrases.

ANOTHER WARNING

In your spliced, added-on and/or dropped-off entries, always make sure the final word reads correctly. It's wise
to have somebody else try them out to make sure your
creation isn't emphasized on the wrong syllable. You
may be surprised to hear your terrific brainchild mispronounced into a meaningless jumble. This "testing" is
particularly important if the name will be spoken, as well
as read—used for a product or announced on radio or
television, for instance. In any event, it pays to read the
name every possible way, just as the judge might interpret it on first reading. And you, yourself, are too close to
it to be objective. I've had names come out sounding
downright unflattering when someone else read it and
was glad I found out before I sent it down the road to
certain failure.

Some winning entries will look good in print only, but
those work out all right when the contest is simply a
prize promotion and not a means to obtain a usable name.

So, now you know how to create prize-winning names.

IS THAT ALL THERE IS?

Not always. Sometimes your name *must* be accompanied
by a short statement explaining it, and sometimes it *may*

be. In either case, naming devices apply to the name, and statement devices apply to the statement (nothing mysterious there). *The Winner Sanctum* will contain both types for your study but a word of—guess what?— *caution:* When you must explain your name, no problem. Write a good statement to go with it, and that's that. On the other hand, when *you* decide to include a statement on your own, either because you feel the name needs clarification or you have such an incredibly fantastic idea for the statement you will explode if you don't include it, you are on thin ground, or shaky ice, or some such mixed-up metaphor.

Two problems with unasked for additions: Are yours necessary because the name itself is so unclear? If so, it might be rejected immediately if judging criteria includes clarity.

But let's assume it's clear, or fairly clear, but you want to submit a statement anyhow. Are you insulting the judge, suggesting he is not wise enough to understand all the intricacies of your name? *Example:* Let's say you named a couple of pigs SHAKESPAIR, and in your statement you mention that Shakespeare wrote HAMLET and that's why it's a good name.

No good. But if you were more subtle (hence, more clever) in your explanation and wrote: "SHAKESPAIR is a good name because baby pigs are little HAMlets," well, that might tickle a judge enough to give you a prizelet, if not the top prize.

If in doubt, and you have enough ideas and enough "qualies," submit some with explanations, some without, as this contester did when she submitted entries in the "Name the Pepsodent Girl" contest. It was a weekly contest, and the same contester had winners two different weeks: LITTLE BOW PEP (4th prize: hi-fi); LITTLE MISS BRUSHET (7th prize: electric shaver).

She also had two losers, and interestingly enough, both losers were sent with accompanying explanations: CLEVERELLA (clean, LEVER Brothers, clever girl because she used Pepsodent); BRIGHTINA (combination of bright and dentine)

Of course, we'll never know if it was merely coincidence that the "explained" names didn't win, or whether the judges felt that if they couldn't stand on their own, they couldn't stand out in the crowd.

REPEATS, REPEATS

Some real or legendary names are naturals for punning and parodies and they show up, over and over, in naming contests. I list them here because I feel it's best to avoid them. However, don't come chasing me if you see them listed somewhere as having won. It may be that some local judges have not tripped over them in entry after entry, and viewed for the first time, they rate high. I'm referring to variations of SIR LANCELOT which can take you from puppies, to turtles, to horses, to frogs to ... whatever ... SIR LAUGHSALOT, SIR JUMP-SALOT, SIR LAGSALOT, SIR WAGSALOT, and on and on.

The same can be said for HOPALONG CASSIDY: HOPSALONG CLASSILY, JUMPSALONG CRAZILY, THUMPSALONG COZILY, MOPESALONG LAZILY, and ...

You get the idea? All right now, be original.

ANATOMY OF A WINNING ENTRY ... OR TWO

The contest was to name the new pony in "Super Circus," a TV show, sponsored by CHUNKY candy. Rules called for a ten-word statement explaining why you chose the name. First prize: a real, live pony.

The contester invented a simple, but excellent, name which was apt for a pony and appropriate for a sponsor whose candy is wrapped in tinfoil: TINFOAL.

Now, admittedly, that's a name that could have been duplicated, and perhaps it was (we'll never know, of course), but her statement obviously carried it, in any event:

Tinfoil keeps freshness in CHUNKY; TINFOAL puts freshness in Super Circus.

Now, that's what she *wanted* to say but—are you counting?—that was eleven words. So, much as she hated to do it, she had to rewrite her statement to get rid of the extra word, the only word totally dispensable: *in*. Her rewritten statement said the same thing but didn't say it as well. Wait, I take that back. It said it very well, indeed. She won the first prize, a live pony. Her statement was:

Tinfoil keeps CHUNKY fresh; TINFOAL puts freshness in "Super Circus."

P.S. It doesn't always happen, but when she told the sponsor she could not accept the pony, they gave her a trip to Bermuda. Ten carefully selected words, that's all it took.

A disc jockey by the name of Bill Thorp ran a contest to name his show. He gave daily prizes of record albums, a weekly prize of a whole bunch of albums, and a grand prize of a trip, or something nice like that. You've already seen one of the daily winners, BILL'S APOPPIN. Here are some more, each one having won for the day it was entered: Spinner Sanctum, THORPedo Junction, Spinner's Circle.

SPINNER SANCTUM was selected as the weekly winner, and I'm wondering if you'll notice anything about that name. If you realized I've called these entry write-ups in each chapter *Winner Sanctum*, you may also realize that I like to play around with *Inner Sanctum*. So, quite naturally, when it came to writing a name for a record show, SPINNER SANCTUM came to me at once (and I *didn't* throw away my first thought because I liked it enough to keep it . . . and there's a lesson there, too).

I wish this story had a bang-up ending, like a big finish with me winning the grand prize. But somebody else did it with—and you have to know the program ended at noon—DESTINATION NOON. A good entry and, as they say, you can't win them all!

THE WINNER SANCTUM

Since these are all "names for," I will leave that out of the description. If I say "Bird sitting on mailbox," the contest called for a name for the bird sitting on the etc. In some cases, I will include the product, but only if it's important to make the winning name understandable.

DEAN'S MILK—*Bird sitting on mailbox:* Baby Twitter (Parody on baby sitter); an apt name because *baby* and *milk* go together.

Fruit-blended cereal for kids (2 winners): Toddler's Woosome (Pun on twosome); Little Bo Peach (Parody) from the same contester who gave you Little Bo Pep; we all have our favorites.

BON AMI Chick: Bleacher's Pet (Parody); name relates well to product, a scouring powder.

Following entries were not keyed because the prize was a bank account (in varying amounts depending on prize won). Contester didn't want to fool around with her name because of a local bank sponsoring it and opening an account for the winners. The challenge was to name a figure of a Scotsman who was saving his money. *One* of these won: Ernie N. Trest (Trik Spelling to make "earn interest"); Laddie Morbucks (Parody); Little Dough Keep (Parody on Little Bo Peep); yes, she wrote Little Bo Peach and Little Bo Pep. Is there no end to this?

Penny Savisearn (Trik Spelling, Splicing, Combo . . . and probably anything else we can think of).

A new dimension is added when pairs (whether it be children, animals, toys, etc.) must be named because you can make the pair of names dependent on each other for meaning. Like so:

Santa's Helpers: TIZTHEE SEASON and TOBY JOLLY
(Fone-et-iks)
(Prize: travel alarm and pen and pencil set)
BOSCO Twins: Lotta Flavor and Benny Ficial (Trik Spelling and Fone-et-iks)
(Prize: toy soldiers)

The following entries won *with explanations,* though explanations were *not* required. Everything (except the notes in parentheses) was part of the entry:

Skyrocket's double: CELESTWIN (Splicing); celestial of the sky-twin
(Prize: camera)
Alcoholic beverage: Tresko (prefix) tres: three ingredients; KO, champ
(Prize: blender)
LA ROSA Rose: FLORIBUNDLE OF JOY (Splicing) Floribunda—a type of rose; bundle of joy—every La Rosa package
(Prize: toys)

And, finally, winning names and statements when statements were *required* as part of the entry:

SUPER COOLA boy, plus letter why you chose name:
I.C. Sparkle (Trik Spelling)—I think this is a good name because when I see my Mommy pouring Super Coola into a glass, my eyes sure sparkle.
(Prize: mechanical robot)

Make up a dessert using COCOA MARSH and name it:
   Milk chocolate lollipop dipped in Cocoa Marsh,
   rolled in colored sprinkles: LOLLIPOPULAR.
   (Name explained previously; go back to page 127).
   (Prize: toys)

7

Cook's Tour of Contestland

If you've been paying attention up to now, you know that no matter what the contest, there are ways to make your entries more outstanding and less likely to be overlooked. Recipe contests are no different, and what's more, you don't have to rely on pot luck. There are ingredients that go into prize-winning entries, and I'm not just talking about flour and sugar. Your destination is the same as in every other contest. You're trying to reach the judge. You take a different route—through your kitchen and his or her stomach—but it's very exciting when you get there because finalists often receive great expense-paid trips to cook-offs and bake-offs where they compete in person with others vying for prizes that really are grand—like Pillsbury's current top prize of $40,000.

WHAT OTHERS? WHO ENTERS?

All kinds of cooks enter—from gourmet to great down-home to good, mediocre, so-so, and "also-cooks." Recipe contests are not always the highly specialized competitions you'd expect them to be. For every entrant who has the ability and talent to create a wholly unusual dish, there are dozens who simply know how to take good basic recipes and make them better and, in the process, turn them into their own original and unique creations. In that respect, cooking contests differ from other skill competitions like photography, sewing, sketching, and the like. It is rare for a novice to come up with a winner in those activities, although the skilled amateur may. But in cooking, it not only *can* happen, it frequently does.

Cooks who normally don't enter contests, and contesters who normally must cook (regardless of deadlines!), find recipe contests a perfect "blending" of two activities. They all want to make those judges sit up and say "More, please."

So, if you've ever tried your hand (with mixing spoon in it) at recipe contests without success, or you've never tried but skim over them the way a good cook skims fat from soup, read on.

We hope to "stir" you up a bit.

STARTING FROM SCRATCH— ANATOMY OF A SPECIAL ENTRY BLANK

Before you dash into your kitchen and start throwing some spices together in a frantic attempt to create a brand new dish, let's take a thorough look at an entry blank (page 141) and go over it rule by rule.

1. *More than $100,000 in prizes:* Nothing to study here. Just thought it would be nice to pause for a minute and think about that expense-paid trip to the Bake-Off. Finalists return home with glowing reports of this memorable experience . . . where cooks are treated like queens—or kings—many men win, too.

THE CATEGORIES

2. *Flour:* Your recipe must use a minimum of one cup of all-purpose, unbleached or self-rising flour. Recipes using the minimum are acceptable, of course, but most of the winners I've seen tend to use more (but then, most cakes do, too, whether contest entry or not). Bear in mind that if you're "forcing" a cup of flour into a recipe to

Front of Pillsbury Bake-Off Entry Blank

Reprinted with permission from the Pillsbury Company.

make it fit the category, you are either in the wrong category or need a better recipe.

3. *Package Mix:* A simple matter of following the rules. The ingredients required are carefully listed, and they ask for "at least one." If you can get more than one into the recipe . . . great! Nobody was ever disqualified for using too much of a sponsor's product—unless it makes for a terrible recipe. Point of interest: You may enter a pie in this category (pie crust mix) or in the flour category (pie from scratch).

4. *Refrigerated Dough:* Again, no question about what they want, but pay attention to those minimum amounts. If you use half a can, you're not following the rules.

RECIPE GROUPS

5. *Special Occasion:* If you decide to enter this group be sure your recipe is definitely a "party-going" kind. It doesn't have to be complicated or elaborate, but it does have to be an "entertaining" dish, the kind you would be proud to serve on an important, hence special, occasion. It must not be family fare.

6. *Ethnic:* An ethnic recipe is either a dish with its roots in some foreign country (tacos, let's say, or Italian pastry) or a domestic recipe in the style of a particular cultural group (Creole cooking, for one). If you're planning to submit such a dish, you would have to make a significant change to make your recipe unique since those that have been handed down from one generation to another are undoubtedly too well known by now to win a contest. Sometimes only one surprising ingredient can do it.

7. *Economy:* Cost-per-serving is an important part of an economy dish. But you must *never* sacrifice nutrition for the sake of economy. Work on both and you may come up with a prizewinner. Also, remember that economy takes in the *total* cost of the dish, so don't start with inexpensive ground beef and then add little bits of lots of exotic ingredients that would shoot the cost way up. If you must have ¼ teaspoon this, ⅛ teaspoon that, those ingredients should be the kind a cook would use in many

different dishes to justify buying them for this recipe.
8. *Note:* See the fine print down there. They are telling
you what they will use when they prepare the *possible*
winners for the home economists to judge. You know, of
course, to use PILLSBURY flour (what is the name of
this Bake-Off?), but because of this little note, it would
make sense to use these brands where applicable. If
you're using mayonnaise, for example, it would be a
smart move to list KRAFT's, rather than HELLMANN's,
right?

On the reverse of the entry blank (page 144), you find:
1. *Your recipe will be judged on the following:*

a) Taste and appearance: Taste goes without saying;
this is, after all, a cooking contest. Appearance is more
important than you might imagine. One winner told me
she was surprised, when she arrived at the Bake-Off, to
find her recipe beautifully photographed, as were all the
other recipes being judged. So make sure your finished
dish can be attractively assembled—and make that an
obvious possibility.

b) Ease of preparation: This does not necessarily mean
your two-ingredient, simple dish; it may have many ingredients, but they should be easy to combine. I would
not consider that numerous ingredients which had to be
sautéed, precooked, parboiled, prebaked before adding
to others would rate very high under "ease of preparation." On the other hand, lots of ingredients that have
only to be measured, mixed or chopped would still qualify. You are the best judge. Are you submitting a recipe
that you would try, even on a busy day, if you stumbled
across it in an ad? Be honest!

c) General availability of ingredients; That's clear. I
recently saw a recipe I was tempted to try, but it called
for Hoisin sauce, and I couldn't find it locally. I didn't
want to go to Chinatown in New York City, so I skipped
the recipe. Maybe some day, when I'm there anyhow,
I'll buy the sauce. But that theory won't get you far in a
recipe contest. The ingredients should be available, and

Enter by October 15, 1979

OFFICIAL RULES FOR THE BAKE-OFF® CONTEST

1. **YOUR RECIPE WILL BE JUDGED ON THE FOLLOWING:**
   - **Taste and appearance**
   - **Ease of preparation**
   - **General availability of ingredients**
   - **Appropriate use of the Category and Group entered**

2. **YOU ARE ELIGIBLE TO ENTER IF:**
   - **You are 10 years of age or older on October 15, 1979, and are a resident of the United States.**

3. **YOU ARE NOT ELIGIBLE TO ENTER AND WILL BE DISQUALIFIED IF:**
   - You are an employee or reside in the household of an employee of The Pillsbury Company, Kraft, Inc., McCormick-Schilling, Standard Brands, or the subsidiaries of any of them, the Range Products Marketing Department of General Electric Company, or the advertising or contest judging agencies of any of the above-mentioned companies.
   - You are a professional, such as a chef, food editor or food home economist, who creates recipes for pay.
   - You, your spouse, your parent, your child, or anyone living in your household have been a finalist in three or more BAKE-OFF® contests or have been a $25,000 BAKE-OFF® contest Grand Prize winner.

4. Recipe must use at least one of the products required for the Category in the quantity specified.

5. Print or type your name, address, telephone number and the Category and Group you are entering on the Entry Blank or plain paper. On a separate sheet, print or type the same information and your recipe.

6. List every ingredient with exact measurements. Give complete directions, pan sizes, baking time and temperature.

7. Mail entries to: BAKE-OFF® Contest, Box 60-38-E, Minneapolis, MN 55460. Entries must be postmarked by October 15, 1979, and received by October 22, 1979. In case of duplicate recipes, the one received first will win. No entries will be acknowledged or returned.

8. Favorite family recipes collected and used over time are eligible as are newly-created recipes. However, in the process of selecting the 100 finalists, Pillsbury will disqualify recipes which it knows to have been previously published in national cookbooks or magazines or by food companies, or those which have been winners in national contests, unless they feature changes which, in its judgment, are significant. Each finalist will be required to certify, on information and belief, that his or her recipe has not been so publicized.

9. Enter as often as desired. No contestant may be a finalist with more than one recipe. Where a recipe qualifies for more than one Category or Group, Pillsbury reserves the right to assign it to that which it thinks best.

10. Initial judging will be done by a professional judging agency and home economists. One hundred finalists will be selected to prepare their recipes in Miami Beach, Florida, on February 25, 1980, for final judging. Each finalist is required to sign a release giving Pillsbury and its nominees full right to use his or her name and likeness for BAKE-OFF® contest-related advertising and publicity. Finalists will be notified by December 15, 1979.

49066-53 20PBI © The Pillsbury Co. 1979

11. In Miami Beach, each recipe must be prepared twice by the finalist alone, exactly as submitted, between 8:00 a.m. and 2:00 p.m.

12. Finalists will compete for 13 cash prizes, consisting of nine $2,000 Group prizes, three $15,000 Category prizes, and one $40,000 Grand prize (consisting of a $15,000 Category prize and a $25,000 First Prize).

13. Rules are binding on all entrants. Judges decisions are final. All entries become the property of The Pillsbury Company, which reserves the right to edit, adapt, use and publish any or all of them.

America's Bake-off Contest

The BAKE-OFF® CONTEST Entry Blank

Pillsbury

Please enter my recipe in the _____ Group

of the _____ Category

Name: _____

Address: _____

City: _____ State: _____ Zip: _____

Telephone Number: Area Code (___) _____

96-2-9E

Back of Pillsbury Bake-Off Entry Blank

Reprinted with permission from the Pillsbury Company.

keep in mind that your recipe must appeal to all sections of the country.

d) Appropriateness for the category and group entered: Even if you have an absolutely smashing lobster dish, don't submit it to the economy group! On the other hand, your plain Jane quickie for busy family night might not be great for company.

2. *You are eligible to enter if:* See how young? Ten years or older. I know several teenagers who've reached the Bake-Off with their own creations. If you see the spark in your son or daughter, encourage it. Some of the most imaginative cooks are young people, and the finest chefs, men.

3. *You are not eligible if:* Read the rules carefully and don't enter if you can't sign a statement that you are eligible under these rules. A cooking teacher asked me if she would be disqualified, and I had to interpret the rule "food home economist who creates recipes for pay" as applying to those who teach cooking.

4. After you create, test, and perhaps change your recipe, *make sure it still complies with the category ingredient rules.* This is an absolute.

5. *Do exactly what it says:* Print or type your name and address; include your telephone number. Even if you use plain paper instead of the entry blank, print or type your recipe on a *separate* sheet of paper, including the information required on the blank. Don't forget to include the category.

6. A recipe contest is no place to say a "pinch" of anything. *Be accurate in all measurements.*

7. *Watch your deadline.*

8. You may start with a recipe from a cookbook and *change it, but don't plagiarize!* You *will* have to sign a statement that your recipe has never been published, but if you've altered an already published one, that's quite acceptable. Some top winners were created that way, as you will see at the end of this chapter.

9. You may submit as many entries as you want, but *you can be a finalist in one group only.*

10. and 11. Before you put a great deal of effort into entering the contest, *be sure you will be available to attend the Bake-Off* if you're a finalist. You must be there, and you will have to prepare your recipe, by yourself, two times.

12. *What nice prizes!*

All right, you've studied the rules and are probably anxious to get going, but *wait!* Keep out of that kitchen until you've finished reading this chapter. First, take a look at some winners.

SOME WINNERS

The following pie was created by a schoolgirl for the 1964 Bake-Off. It won $25,000.

PEACHEESY PIE

CRUST

2 cups Pillsbury's Best® All Purpose or Unbleached Flour*
1 teaspoon salt
⅔ cup shortening
6 to 7 tablespoons reserved peach syrup

PEACH FILLING

29 -oz. can cling peach slices, drained (reserve syrup)
2 tablespoons sugar
2 tablespoons cornstarch
2 tablespoons corn syrup
1 to 2 teaspoons pumpkin pie spice
2 teaspoons vanilla
2 tablespoons margarine or butter

CHEESECAKE TOPPING

2 eggs, slightly beaten
⅓ cup sugar
1 tablespoon lemon juice
2 tablespoons peach syrup
3 -oz. pkg. cream cheese, softened
½ cup dairy sour cream

Heat oven to 425°F. (Lightly spoon flour into measuring cup; level off.) In medium bowl, combine flour and salt. Using pastry blender or mixer at low speed, cut in shortening until mixture is size of small peas. Sprinkle peach syrup over mixture while tossing and mixing lightly with fork. Add syrup until dough is just moist enough to hold together. Divide dough in half. Form each half into a ball; place half on floured surface. Flatten ball slightly; smooth edges. Roll out dough to a circle 1½ inches larger than inverted 9-inch pie pan. Fold pastry in half; place in pan and unfold, easing into pan. Trim edge of pastry 1 inch from rim of pan; fold pastry under, even with rim, and flute.

In medium bowl, combine all Filling ingredients except margarine. Pour into pastry shell. Dot with margarine. In small saucepan, combine eggs, ⅓ cup sugar, lemon juice and 2 tablespoons peach syrup. Cook, stirring constantly until thick. In medium bowl, blend cream cheese and sour cream until smooth. Add hot mixture; beat until smooth. Spread Topping over Peach Filling.

Roll out remaining dough. Cut into 2-inch circles. Brush with peach syrup. Arrange on Topping. Bake at 425°F. for 7 minutes. Cover edge with foil, then bake at 350°F. for 30 to 35 minutes or until crust is deep golden brown. Store in refrigerator.

9-inch pie

TIPS:
* If using Pillsbury's Best® Self Rising Flour, omit salt.
● A pastry cloth and stockinette-covered rolling pin makes pastry rolling easier.

HIGH ALTITUDE: No change.

Reprinted from Pillsbury Bake-Off® Classics. Copyright © 1979 by the Pillsbury Company.

The following cake, although not a Grand Prize winner did take its creator to the all-expense-paid Bake-Off in 1965, and it's still a favorite.

TUNNEL OF FUDGE CAKE

1½ cups margarine or
    butter, softened
 6 eggs
1½ cups sugar
 2 cups Pillsbury's Best®
    All Purpose or
    Unbleached Flour*

3⅓ cups Pillsbury Rich 'N
    Easy® Creamy Double
    Dutch Frosting Mix**
    (save remaining mix
    for glaze, if desired)
 2 cups chopped walnuts
    or pecans

Heat oven to 350°F. Generously grease (not oil) 12-cup fluted tube pan or 10-inch tube pan (non-stick finish pan, too). In large bowl, cream margarine. Add eggs, one at a time, beating well after each. Gradually add sugar, creaming until light and fluffy. By hand, stir in flour, dry frosting mix and walnuts until well blended. Pour batter into prepared pan. Bake at 350°F. for 60 to 65 minutes. Since this cake has the soft tunnel of fudge, ordinary doneness tests cannot be used. Test after 60 minutes by observing a dry, shiny brownie-type crust. Cool upright in pan to lukewarm; turn onto serving plate. Cool completely.

For glaze, blend remaining frosting mix and 4 teaspoons water until smooth. If necessary, add few drops of water to make glaze consistency. Spoon over cooled cake. Store cake under airtight cover. 10-inch ring cake

TIPS:
  * Self-rising flour not recommended.
** Rich 'N Easy® Creamy Double Dutch Frosting Mix or Rich 'N Easy® Creamy Fudge Frosting Mix and walnuts or pecans are essential to the success of this recipe.

HIGH ALTITUDE: Above 3500 Feet: Bake at 375°F. for 60 to 65 minutes.

Reprinted from Pillsbury Bake-Off® Classics. Copyright © 1979 by the Pillsbury Company.

And for a refrigerated dough winner (in the twenty-fifth Bake-Off) here is an entirely different kind of recipe. Try it; you'll like it (the judges did: $25,000 worth).

SAVORY CRESCENT
CHICKEN SQUARES

3 -oz. pkg. cream cheese,
   softened
3 tablespoons margarine
   or butter, melted
2 cups cooked cubed
   chicken or two 5-oz.
   cans boned chicken
¼ teaspoon salt
⅛ teaspoon pepper
2 tablespoons milk

1 tablespoon chopped
   chives or onion
1 tablespoon chopped
   pimiento, if desired
8 -oz. can Pillsbury
   Refrigerated Quick
   Crescent Dinner Rolls
¾ cup seasoned croutons,
   crushed

Heat oven to 350°F. In medium bowl, blend cream cheese and 2 tablespoons margarine (reserve 1 tablespoon) until smooth. Add the next 6 ingredients; mix well. Separate crescent dough into 4 rectangles; firmly press perforations to seal. Spoon ½ cup meat mixture onto center of each rectangle. Pull 4 corners of dough to top center of chicken mixture, twist slightly and seal edges. Brush tops with reserved 1 tablespoon margarine; dip in crouton crumbs. Place on ungreased cookie sheet. Bake at 350°F. for 20 to 25 minutes or until golden brown.

4 sandwiches

HIGH ALTITUDE: No change.

Reprinted from Pillsbury Bake-Off® Classics. Copyright © 1979 by the Pillsbury Company.

Now that you've seen the caliber of these winning entries, it's time to ask yourself some questions. Your *honest* answers will tell you if you should be entering recipe contests, or trying to win enough in statement contests to eat out a lot. Ready?

CAN YOU WHIP UP WINNERS?

	YES	NO
• Do you love to experiment in the kitchen?	____	____
• Do you *always* follow a recipe as is?	____	____
• Can you change some ingedients to suit your own, and your family's, taste?	____	____
• If you make changes, are your combinations usually the right ones?	____	____
• Do your guests often ask, "whatever did you put in here?"—and they mean it in a complimentary way?	____	____
• Can you combine *unlikely* ingredients and have them come out *likable?*	____	____
• Can you—*dare* you?—feed the results of your experiments to your family?	____	____
• Are they honest enough to tell you what they really think (don't worry if you have kids; they'll tell you *exactly* what they think!)?	____	____
• Would you rather cook a frozen dinner than prepare a real meal?	____	____
• Are you the kind of cook who leaves a little something out of a recipe when giving it to a friend? (Naughty! Naughty!)	____	____
• When you do give a complete recipe, are your measurements accurate?	____	____
• Or do you say, "Add enough water until the consistency looks right"?	____	____
• Could you go to a Bake-Off and prepare your dish under lights, under pressure, under the eyes of the judges?	____	____
• And if you are a big winner, will you be happy cooking that recipe over and over for all your friends and family who will expect you to invite them for lunch and dinner forever because, after all, you're a prizewinning cook?	____	____

Scoring: There is none for this quiz. By now, you know if you want to enter recipe contests, and I'll assume that you have "measured up" and are still anxious to get into the kitchen.

MEASURING UP

Measuring ingredients really is serious business. Remember, those reading your recipe for the first time have no idea what it should look like or what its consistency is meant to be. That goes not only for judges but for every consumer who will see the winning entry and want to try it. Every time you try a new combination you must *measure!* Every single ingredient must be accounted for down to the tiniest ⅛ of a teaspoon. Every good cookbook will tell you how to measure correctly; if you've been a "little of this" and a "little of that" kind of cook up to now, start doing it the right way . . . so when you come to the "write" way, you can submit an entry the judges will be happy to pass on to the home economists for taste-testing.

If you leave the all-important measurements out, your entry won't even get past the preliminary judge.

WHAT ELSE GOES INTO A PRIZEWINNING RECIPE

I'm not talking about the flour, the sugar, the two eggs, well beaten. I'll leave that to you. What I am talking about is everything else that goes into your recipe, like the kind, the name, the presentation.

We're back, once again, to following the rules. If they want casseroles, don't think you can be different and submit your absolutely fantastic recipe that will knock them for a loop . . . and so what if it's made in an electric skillet; it's so terrific they'll have to give it a prize.

They won't!

Look at this *Busy People's Recipe Contest* conducted by *Better Homes & Gardens* magazine.

BUSY PEOPLE'S RECIPE CONTEST

Are you involved in a daily race with the clock as you try to cook nutritious family meals and keep up with myriad other activities? If so, we're hoping you've come up with some timesaving recipes that help you cope. Send them to us, and you might win $2,000 or 27 other top prizes.

1st PRIZE $2,000
2nd PRIZE $1,000
3rd PRIZE $750
4th PRIZE through 28th PRIZE $250
100 honorable mentions will receive the *Better Homes and Gardens®
Complete Step-by-Step Cook Book*

To start you thinking: Have you streamlined a favorite but time-consuming recipe into a fast-to-fix one? Do you give a new twist to a convenience food to short-cut meal preparation? Are timesaving appliances such as the slow cooker or microwave oven a part of your cooking repertoire? Is your favorite recipe one you can quickly prepare, then put in the oven and forget? If you have recipes you'd like to share, send them to us. You might be a big winner. Hints: chicken and vegetable stir-fry, minute steak barbecue, easy ravioli soup, lazy daisy coffee cake, no-bake peach petal pie.

RULES FOR ENTERING THIS CONTEST

1. Print clearly or type your name and address on the entry blank provided. Check the category into which your recipe falls. If a special appliance is needed to prepare your recipe, note this on the form also. (This is for our sorting purposes only. A top prizewinner will not necessarily be chosen from each category.)

2. Write or type each Busy People's Recipe on a plain sheet of paper. Write or type your full name and address on each paper in the upper right-hand corner. Enter as many recipes as you wish, but write each entry on a separate piece of paper.

3. Give all measurements in level cups, tablespoons, teaspoons.

4. Specify brand names of nationally known food products you use as ingredients, so we can test your recipe with the same brands.

5. Include a statement of not more than 50 words explaining the recipe origin and why it is timesaving.

6. Entries will be judged on originality, taste, appearance, and clarity. Decisions of the judges will be final.

7. Mail entries to Busy People's Recipe Contest, P.O. Box 10623, Des Moines, Iowa 50336. All entries must be postmarked no later than May 1, 1979, and received by May 15, 1979.

8. If your recipe is judged a winner, you give Meredith Corporation the right to use it in any manner as long as we wish. We reserve the right to adjust and edit recipes. Contest winners will be notified in August, 1979.

9. All winners will be required to sign an affidavit certifying that their entries are original ideas, not previously published, and that they have followed these official contest rules.

10. A list of winners may be obtained by sending a self-addressed stamped envelope. No recipes will be returned.

11. Any resident of the United States or Canada may enter. Employees of Meredith Corporation, its affiliates, subsidiaries, its advertising agencies, and their families, are not eligible.

12. The top winning entries will be published in a future issue of *Better Homes and Gardens®* magazine.

13. This contest is subject to all federal, state, and local laws and regulations. All liability for federal, state, or other taxes imposed on a prizewinner are the sole responsibility of each winner and not of Meredith Corporation. This contest is void where prohibited by law.

ENTRY BLANK
Busy People's Recipe Contest
P.O. Box 10623
Des Moines, Iowa 50336

My recipe is:

☐ Dessert

☐ Main Dish

   ☐ Meat

   ☐ Poultry

   ☐ Fish and Seafood

   ☐ Eggs and Cheese

☐ Salad

☐ Soup

☐ Vegetable

☐ Bread and Sandwich

☐ Appetizer and Snack

Check if applicable:
My recipe requires:

☐ Microwave Oven

☐ Slow Cooker

☐ Blender

☐ Food Processor

Name of recipe: _____

Your name: _____

Address: _____

City: _____ State: _____ Zip: _____

Notice how many different types of dishes may be submitted, and how many different methods of cooking. Of course, not all contests are this explicit, but when they are, that means you must be, too.

There was a recent contest run for "Summer Dishes," so entries would naturally have to be particularly appealing on a hot, sticky summer's day. *They're* being specific; the *entry* must be specific. As in every other contest, you must give them what they want.

BACK TO "MAKING A STATEMENT"

Look at rule 5 in the *Busy People's Recipe Contest: Include a statement of not more than 50 words explaining the recipe origin and why it is timesaving.*

A good statement won't help a bad recipe, but a good recipe can be helped a lot by an impressive statement. So if the rules call for one, write it up as carefully as if you were entering a statement contest. Go back to basics, and sprinkle in a few devices, sparingly.

If a statement is not required but not excluded by the rules, and you feel you have *something important* to say about your recipe, such as its origin or the many ways it can be used, or its unusual nutritional wallop, then by all means, include it.

The following recipe was entered in a COLLEGE INN® Chicken Broth contest. No statement was called for, but the young woman who created the recipe did have an important comment to make, and she made it so well that she won a U.S. Savings Bond.

First the recipe, then the statement.

LICKITY-CHICK LASAGNA

Preparation time: approximately 45 minutes
Cooking Time: approximately 25 minutes

 2 13-¾ oz. cans COLLEGE INN® Chicken Broth
 1 cup water

Recipe and statement reprinted with permission of College Inn®, a registered trademark of RJR Foods, Inc., Winston-Salem, N.C.

1 lb. boned chicken breasts (chicken cutlets)
2 pkgs. chopped frozen spinach
2 cans refrigerated crescent dinner rolls
1 lb. ricotta cheese
1 egg
⅓ cup grated Parmesan cheese
8 oz. mozzarella cheese, sliced
4 tb. butter
4 tb. flour
1 4-oz. can mushrooms (stems and pieces)
¼ tsp. salt
⅛ tsp. pepper

Add water to chicken broth and bring to boil. Simmer chicken breasts in broth until tender, about 30 minutes. While chicken is simmering, cook spinach according to directions and drain thoroughly. Set aside. Mix together ricotta cheese, Parmesan cheese and egg, and set aside. Remove cooked chicken breases and dice or shred. Reserve broth.

Melt butter in saucepan. Stir in flour. Add reserved broth slowly, stirring until boiling, smooth and thickened. Add chicken, mushrooms, salt and pepper to broth.

Separate rolls into eight rectangles. Place on cookie sheet, one slightly overlapping the other, to form a 15- x 13-inch rectangle. Press edges of dough and perforations together to seal. Down center of long side, layer half of spinach to within 1½ inches of both 13-inch ends. Layer half of ricotta mixture on top of spinach. Then add a layer of chicken mixture. Top with layer of mozzarella. Repeat layers once more. Fold 13-inch sides of dough over filling for 1½ inches. Then bring long sides of dough over filling, overlapping edges slightly. Pinch to seal. Bake at 375 degrees for 25 minutes, until golden brown. Slice to serve, topping with any leftover chicken sauce.

And now, the statement, which was added at the end of the recipe:

Note: I think my recipe is special because the roll-crust is quicker, easier, and better tasting than lasagna noodles. But what is really original and special and good and good for you is the idea of a chicken-spinach-cheese lasagna. You can serve your protein, your vegetable, and your bread in one dish, with College Inn full-strength broth giving everything a chickeny-wonderful taste!

I can hear you saying "Wow!" which is exactly how I reacted when I first heard this statement. It was a creative, imaginative recipe with a creative, imaginative statement. Who can say which carried more weight, although neither could have won all by itself.

Even its name—*Lickity-Chick Lasagna*—added to the appeal of the entire entry.

AND SPEAKING OF NAMES

It *is* vital to give your recipe an attractive name, one that will make the preliminary judge—the first judge to read your recipe—want to see what it's all about. You can't be overly clever (thus, obscure) nor can you be too unimaginative. As in all other naming contests, you must walk the fine line. Which, by the way, is an excellent approach to naming your recipe. Think of it as one of those "somethings" to be named and treat it as you would any other naming contest. Think of the recipe names you've seen here: *Peacheesy Pie, Tunnel of Fudge, Savory Crescent Squares, Lickity-Chick Lasagna* (employing Pun, Parody, Spelling Triks, Alliteration, Splicing). Any could have been winners in a straight naming contest.

The name should tell something about the dish, of course. If there is an unusual point you want to make immediately, the name is the place to do it. One Pillsbury winner added sesame seeds to her pie crust (now, that's unique!) and called her single-crust creation *Open Sesame Pie.* If *I* were reading entries, I'd want to know how a pie came to be called *Open Sesame*, wouldn't you?

The Shepherd Contest Course lists some great names, along with some winning recipes, in the chapter on recipe contests. I've taken a few of these names and without giving you the actual name, just clues and naming devices, I'd like you to take *Your Turn* and create names with the information given. The real names will be at the end of the chapter, but yours might be just as good . . . or better.

YOUR TURN

Example: A cheese omelet submitted to a QUAKER OATS contest (with, obviously, QUAKER OATS as one of the ingredients). Naming device—Splicing, Coined Word: CHEESE OMELOATS

1. Dish containing tunafish, apples, and a form of the word "tease" coined for this name. Naming devices —Splicing, Alliteration, Coined Word:

   (2 words) _____

2. Casserole of tunafish and tomatoes. Device—Splicing

   (2 words) _____

3. Buns made with cinnamon, mince, and cider. Devices —Splicing, Alliteration:

   (3 words) _____

4. A simple apple pudding with not much more in the name than a rhyming device:

   (3 words) _____

5. A dish that's baked with beans, appealing to teenagers. Devices—Inner Rhyme and Alliteration:

   (3 words) _____

It is perfectly acceptable to add a subtitle to your name if you feel it will help, as this $25,000 winner did in a Pillsbury contest: RING-A-LINGS (*Sweet Nut Rolls*).

An entry blank for the National Chicken Cooking Contest included a sample recipe which called for applesauce to be poured over chicken before baking. Its name: SIMPLE SAUCY CHICKEN.

Remember, the first impression the judge gets of your entry is its name. Give him something to be impressed with and he may return the favor!

WHAT ELSE MAKES AN IMPRESSION?

Following the rules, that's what. Especially the rules which tell how the entries will be judged. You've already seen some of the judging standards, and they will be repeated here along with other criteria you haven't come across yet . . . but you will.

Taste and *appearance* don't need too much explaining, except to add that sometimes the way you shape your dish can add to its appearance. A winner in a Pillsbury Bake-Off made her own baking pan by accordian-pleating aluminum foil and calling her cookies thus baked ACCORDIAN TREATS.

Ease of preparation is almost the same as *simplicity* (an often-seen judging standard). They both call for a dish that can be put together easily by the average home cook in a reasonable amount of time. In my opinion, *simplicity* goes even further: not too many ingredients; few pots and pans to clean up; using one ingredient that can take the place of three (pancake mix instead of three different kinds of flour, for example). Since people's conception of what is simple varies according to circumstances, it is best to let the type of contest and the rest of the criteria guide you. Are the recipes for working mothers? For party-fare? For take-along lunches? Pay attention to those not-so-hidden clues.

Appeal, simply stated, means that your recipe should be appealing. *Appeal* and *appearance* are not entirely interchangeable although they sometimes may be. Remember, the sponsor may very well be looking for recipes to feature in ads or on labels. Will yours *appeal to a majority of people?* If you happen to adore onions in your ice cream, that's your business; just don't try to pass it off as an appealing recipe. The appearance of your dish might also appeal to people, and that's when the two cross over.

Creativity and *originality* are interchangeable, and one or the other is usually very high up in judging criteria. As I mentioned before, you *are* original when you substitute ingredients, add some, or take some out. Whenever you change a recipe substantially to make it your own, you are being original and creative. This includes taking well-known basic recipes and doing all sorts of creative things with them. Make sure that you will be able to sign an affidavit that the recipe is original because you will frequently have to do just that. But taking a published recipe, for example, and simply changing the brand of bread crumbs does not come under the heading of creativity.

Appropriateness of idea means that you're not sending in a recipe for *Pressed Duck* to a Working Mother Recipe Contest, or worse, to the National Chicken Cooking Contest. It's easy to be appropriate if you stop and think about what you're submitting where.

Quality comes up now and then, but I think you should keep quality in mind even when it isn't mentioned. Quality of ingredients (which does not mean expensive, but good) and quality of nutrition—very important.

Practicality, though not often mentioned specifically, is an important "ingredient" in most recipe contests . . . with the exception of gourmet-type cooking where truffles as an important part of the recipe would seem quite natural. For most folks, getting truffles would involve a long search and prohibitive expense. Ingredients should be readily available, and the recipe should be practical for the type of people likely to use it. "Cooking for Two" should not inspire you to submit a *Beef Wellington,* for example, since a whole *filet mignon* would be one of the *impractical* ingredients . . . unless guests were expected, and then it would no longer be Cooking for Two. See?

If you stop to think about the kind of contest you're entering, you will find that interpreting the rules is really quite easy.

INTO THE KITCHEN

Once you've determined what recipe you're going to submit, or what variations you're going to try, give yourself plenty of time to kitchen-test your creations. Pretend you're doing them for a company dinner because you will want the final dish to be picture pretty (remember *appearance*). Make notes as you go along. If the recipe did not come out just as you expected, go back over your notes to see what ingredients need correcting. If at first you don't succeed, *fry, fry, again!*

Now you're ready to write it up.

WRITE IT UP

Neatness counts. Let's face it, reading recipe after recipe is second in excitement to reading the phone book. Do everything you can to make it easy for the judge to read yours. Type your entries, if possible, or print very neatly on clean white paper. Put the title at the top, centered, in capital letters (subtitle, if necessary, in parentheses right below). Don't crowd your letters.

Under the title comes the list of ingredients, *in the order in which they will be used,* and with measurements clearly indicated. Type or print the sponsor's brand name in caps. He deserves the recognition. It's all right to mention another noncompetitive brand by name if it's important to the recipe. If you think a certain brand of seasoned bread crumbs enchances your recipe, include the brand name. Again, you just want to give yourself every advantage, and short of being there to cook it yourself, you must help them duplicate your exact recipe.

Now, write it up. Be sure to include everything, down to the little details, you want the cook—be it contest judge, home economist or next door neighbor—to know and do. There is no place in cooking contests for the "Oops, I forgot to tell you" approach to recipe swapping. Should they preheat the oven? Tell them right up front. Sprinkle flour in the pan? Don't forget to mention it. Leave nothing to the imagination, but at the same time keep your directions as clear and succinct as possible. You don't have to go into great detail about the "how." Don't say, for example, "Pour applesauce over the chicken in the pan before you put the pan in the oven." If you've already told them how to arrange the chicken in the pan, you can simply direct them to "Pour applesauce over chicken."

Part of your write-up will, of course, include the method of cooking or baking (size of utensil, for instance). This can be so important that finalists at some major Cook-Offs and Bake-Offs are permitted to bring their own equipment. Otherwise, they will use (and usually keep) new ones supplied by the sponsor. Certainly, if you've created some special kind of item for the recipe, as one Pillsbury winner did when she formed her cookies into a "T" with a homemade cookie cutter, you'd better take good care of it. You might be taking it on an expense-paid trip to Bake-Off city.

Since duplication is as much a problem in recipe contests as in any other, give yourself a better chance by submitting more than one entry, unless the rules state otherwise. One consistent winner says she usually submits about a dozen to one contest. Don't forget, a losing entry in one contest might be a winner in another.

Anyhow, you can't really lose, no matter what. If you write a twenty-five word statement and it doesn't win, what do you have? Just a twenty-five word statement that may or may not work in another contest. But if you cook up a spectacular dish that doesn't win . . . well, at least you have a spectacular dish that wins in your kitchen.

By now, you are, I hope, eager to really get into the kitchen and start whipping up some of those prize-winning recipes.

WIN A TWO-WEEK SAFARI

12th Annual
Reader Recipe Contest
36 Prizes

Nairobi Hilton (left) provides indoor and outdoor excitement

At Salt Lick Lodge (bottom), view game close-up

The Grand Prize

A dream vacation for two: a safari to Kenya. You and your guest will fly on British Airways, the airline that takes good care of you, to Nairobi where twin accommodations will await you at the Nairobi Hilton. Then on to Kenya for the safari, with accommodations at the Hilton International Taita Hills Game Lodge and Salt Lick. (This offer does not include meals, is contingent on space availability and expires within one year of notification.) Please turn page for more prizes.

Reprinted by permission of Weight Watchers® *magazine.*

HERE ARE THE JUDGES

Richard Grausman is the U.S. representative of Le Cordon Bleu; conducts cooking classes in major cities.

Arno Schmidt is executive chef of NY's Waldorf-Astoria Hotel; member of international culinary societies.

Jeanne Goldberg is a nutritionist and columnist; lecturer at Tufts University, Medford, MA.

Lee Haiken is food editor for *Weight Watchers Magazine*; member of the Cordon Bleu, NY.

James Coco is an actor who has worked in every media; will soon have his first book published.

1. Every recipe must meet the requirements of the Weight Watchers Food Program.

2. *Weight Watchers Magazine*'s Twelfth Annual Reader Recipe Contest is open to anyone in the United States and Canada except employees of the following: Weight Watchers International, Inc., their affiliated companies and advertising agencies; *Weight Watchers Magazine* and American/Harlequin and their advertising agencies; advertisers supplying prizes for the contest and their advertising agencies; or anyone in the weight-control business. This offer is void in areas where prohibited by law.

3. There is no entry charge.

4. Recipes must be typed or handwritten legibly. Please print the category you are entering (Legal or Maintenance), name of recipe, time served (morning, midday, or evening meal, or snack), and number of servings clearly at the top of each page, on standard paper (8½" x 11").

5. Contestant's name and address, including ZIP code and phone number, must appear plainly on top of each recipe sheet.

6. A photo of the finalists may be requested. If used, this photo becomes the property of *Weight Watchers Magazine*, which has the right to publish the photo.

7. Recipes will be judged on originality, taste and practicality.

8. Prizes will be awarded as listed, with no substitutions, and decisions of the judges will be final. If a particular prize is not available at time of judging, a similar prize of equal value will be substituted.

9. All recipes submitted become the property of *Weight Watchers Magazine*, which has the right to edit the material in any way and to publish the recipes as well as winners' names and addresses.

10. Entries should be addressed to Recipe Contest, *Weight Watchers Magazine*, 149 Fifth Avenue, New York, NY 10010. They must be postmarked no later than midnight November 15, 1979. The sponsor is not responsible for entries lost or unduly delayed in the mails.

CONTEST CATEGORIES

1. **Legal:** All recipes must be original. Any recipe conforming to the basic Weight Watchers Food Program will be judged in this category. Recipes must meet requirements of the Weight Watchers Food Program.

Example:
Reprint from May 1979 issue:

CURRIED LAMB AND EGGPLANT BAKE
Leslie Ayres
San Francisco, CA

1 cup thinly sliced pared carrots
2 ounces onion, chopped
3 small garlic cloves, minced
1 cup tomato purée
¾ cup buttermilk
1 medium tomato, diced
1 tablespoon curry powder
1 teaspoon cumin
2 bay leaves
½ teaspoon each salt and fennel seed
¼ teaspoon oregano
1 medium eggplant
12 ounces cooked ground lamb, crumbled
1 cup cooked enriched rice

In a large nonstick skillet, cook carrots, onion and garlic about 5 minutes or until onions are soft. Add next 8 ingredients and mix well; simmer, stirring occasionally, 15 minutes. While tomato mixture is cooking, prepare eggplant. Cut eggplant in half lengthwise and scoop out the pulp, leaving the shell intact; reserve the eggplant shells and cut the pulp into ½" cubes. Add the eggplant cubes to the tomato mixture and stir to combine; continue to simmer 10 minutes longer. Remove and discard bay leaves. Add the lamb and rice and mix well. Stuff each eggplant shell with ½ of the lamb and eggplant mixture. Place on a baking sheet and bake at 350° F. about 35 minutes or until the eggplant shells are tender. Makes 2 servings. (Evening Meal)

2. **Maintenance:** All recipes must be original. Any recipe in the Maintenance Plan category must carry a Unit designation (50 calories per unit) and will be judged on its adaptability to the Maintenance Plan. No recipe exceeding 8 Units (400 calories) per serving will be considered.

Example:
Reprint from November 1978 issue:
Step into Week 2 of your Maintenance Plan with a creamy, chocolaty, dessert. The surprise? This delicious cake fits into your daily Menu Plan with the Maintenance Plan addition of just 2 plain graham crackers (5" x 2½"), approximately 50 calories each, per serving.

ICEBOX CHOCOLATE PIE

1 tablespoon + 1 teaspoon unsweetened cocoa
1⅛ teaspoons arrowroot
⅛ teaspoon salt
½ cup skim milk, scalded
2 medium eggs, separated
3 tablespoons granulated sugar replacement, divided
½ cup evaporated skimmed milk
1 teaspoon vanilla extract
4 plain graham crackers (5" x 2½" each) made into crumbs

Sift cocoa, arrowroot and salt together into the top of a double boiler. Blend in skim milk; stir in egg yolks and 2 tablespoons sugar replacement. Place top of double boiler over boiling water and cook, stirring constantly, 2-3 minutes or until thickened. Remove from heat and cool. In a medium bowl, beat egg whites, remaining sugar replacement, evaporated skimmed milk and vanilla until stiff; fold into cooled cocoa mixture. Spread half of the graham cracker crumbs in 9" nonstick pie pan; pour in cocoa mixture. Sprinkle remaining crumbs evenly over the top. Freeze until firm. Makes 2 Maintenance Plan servings. (Midday Meal) (Supplement as required.)

continued on page 56

RECIPE CONTEST

continued

CONTEST RECIPE GUIDELINES

Keep these tips in mind when writing your recipe:

1. List ingredients in the order in which they are used.

2. Use measurements based on standard measuring cups and spoons.

3. Specify correct means of measure by cup (volume) or scale (weight).

4. Give directions step-by-step in short sentences.

5. Indicate oven temperature where applicable.

6. Give sizes of utensils and cookware, and directions for special equipment.

7. All recipes should be based on servings for women, i.e., meat, fish and poultry should not exceed six ounces cooked weight. Some cheeses are permitted in amounts of up to ⅔ cup for soft and no more than two ounces for hard or semisoft cheese. The maximum ounces allowed per serving for such legumes as dried beans, lentils or peas is eight ounces cooked weight.

8. Use fresh, canned or frozen fruits, no sugar added.

9. Enriched white or whole grain breads are permitted; each serving must not exceed one ounce.

10. Skim milk, nonfat dry milk, evaporated skimmed milk, buttermilk and plain, unflavored yogurt may be used.

11. Some vegetables are limited to four ounces daily, such as onions, peas and water chestnuts.

12. Fats which may be used are margarine, imitation (or diet) margarine, mayonnaise, imitation mayonnaise and vegetable oil.

13. In the preparation of recipes, you may use up to three servings daily of such items as cornstarch (1 tsp.), flour (1 tsp.), bouillon (1 cube or 1 tsp.), catsup (2 tsp.), unsweetened cocoa (1 tsp.), unflavored gelatin (½ packet) and yeast extract (1 tsp.). Amounts listed are per serving. Spoon measurements must be level.

CONTEST COOKING PROCEDURES

Basically, the method of cooking involves boiling, broiling, baking or roasting on a rack. Such items as poultry, fish or liver may be poached or pan-broiled as well. Raw ground meat maybe combined with other ingredients if boiled, or baked on a rack. Cooked legumes may be mixed with other ingredients. Fats may be baked in a casserole with other ingredients but may never be used in sautéing or frying.

Maintenance Plan recipes may be prepared by any method.

BUT FIRST, A WORD FOR THE SPONSOR

Not only are recipe contests enormously appealing to the public but to advertisers as well. They find these contests the best kind of prize promotion. After all, what better way to bring new recipes to the attention of the public than to bring the public in to create the new recipes! It's like asking a salesman to go out and give a sales pitch . . . to himself. For the price of some prizes—albeit very large ones, in many cases—the sponsor "hires" thousands of "cooks" to test his product in their own kitchens and write out a report (the entry). He can then publish the best results (the winners) in booklets, on labels, in magazine and newspaper ads, and everybody comes out ahead, especially the consumer.

That's why some very fine companies have been running regular contests for years. Pillsbury Bake-Offs have been going on since 1949 and show no signs of letting

COOK YOUR WAY TO FAME.

Win the recognition you deserve.
We invite you to enter
The Christian Brothers® Annual Sherry Recipe Contest.

WIN
FOUR FIRST PRIZES:
$1000 Cash Each — plus lavish weekends for two in San Francisco.

WIN
CELEBRITY RECOGNITION:
As a First Prize winner you will be honored at a gala banquet atop San Francisco's Nob Hill, featuring your recipe prepared by an internationally famed chef.

WIN
1000 HONORABLE MENTION PRIZES:
One-year subscriptions to Bon Appétit Magazine.

IT'S EASY TO ENTER:
All you have to do is send us your favorite original recipe using any one of The Christian Brothers premium California Sherries. There are four categories: Appetizers, Soups, Entrees and Desserts. Each category has a First Prize winner. It could be your recipe!

The Christian Brothers make 5 premium California Sherries — Choose one for your recipe.

Cocktail Sherry
The lightest and driest. Its classic nutlike taste adds character to recipes. Delicious chilled or over ice.

Dry Sherry
Pale gold, light-bodied and dry with a fine, smooth flavor. Excellent before meals and to use in a variety of dishes.

Golden Sherry
A delightful "medium" Sherry — a bit sweeter than Dry, yet not as rich as Cream. A preferred taste for many occasions.

Cream Sherry
Rich and smooth, with a true creamy quality and golden amber color. Enjoy it chilled, over ice, or in recipes.

Meloso Cream Sherry
A truly luxurious Sherry with honey-like character. Produced only in limited quantities by The Christian Brothers of California.

Here are the official rules for entering The Christian Brothers Sherry Recipe Contest:

1) You may enter as often as you wish. Each entry must be on a separate sheet of paper and clearly marked for either Appetizer, Soup, Entree, or Dessert. A First Prize winner will be chosen in each of these four categories. An Honorable Mention prize will be awarded to the next best one thousand recipes as determined by the judges.

2) Your recipe must be typed or plainly printed and must specify all ingredients and steps clearly

3) Your recipe must include one of The Christian Brothers Sherries as an ingredient. NO PURCHASE IS REQUIRED

4) Entries must be postmarked no later than December 31, 1979, and received by January 15, 1980. Judging will be completed by April 1, 1980, and the four major winners will be notified by April 15, 1980.

5) All entries will be judged by Maggie's Kitchen. Recipes will be evaluated on the basis of originality, imaginative use of sherry and taste, as well as the listing of ingredients, proper measurements, and clarity of directions. Decisions of the judges are final. No correspondence will be answered.

6) PRIZES: Four first prizes, one-weekend vacations for two in San Francisco, May 16 through May 18, 1980, plus $1,000 per prize winner. One thousand honorable mention prizes: one-year subscriptions to Bon Appétit Magazine.

7) Recipe entries may not have been previously published or otherwise restricted legally. All entries become the property of The Christian Brothers and none will be returned. Submission of a recipe in this contest gives The Christian Brothers the right to adapt and publish the recipe without further compensation to the entrant, whether or not contest is prohibited by law.

8) All prizes will be awarded and none are transferable. Taxes on prizes are the responsibility of the winners. The odds of winning are a function of the number of suitable entries received.

9) Winners will be notified by mail. A list of major winners will be sent after June 15, 1980, to anyone who sends a stamped, self-addressed envelope by January 15, 1980, to: Recipe Contest Winners, P.O. Box 99607, San Francisco, CA 94109.

10) Contest is open to all residents of the United States who are of legal drinking age under the laws of their home states. Affidavits may be required of the winners. The following persons are not eligible: members of the Order of the Brothers of the Christian Schools, employees of the following organizations and their families: Mont La Salle Vineyards, Fromm and Sichel, Inc., Maggie's Kitchen, their advertising and merchandising agencies, liquor and wine wholesalers and retailers, federal and state liquor and wine authorities, Bon Appétit Magazine. This contest is void in the following states: AL, CA, CO, GA, IA, MI, NJ, OH, OK, PA, TX, UT, VA, and other states or localities where illegal or otherwise restricted by law.

11) Mail entries to:
The Christian Brothers Sherry Recipe Contest
P.O. Box 7461 Dept.
San Francisco, California 94120

◁ *Antoine B. Huber, Maître de Cuisine of The Mark Hopkins, An Inter-Continental Hotel, San Francisco, displays the prize-winning dishes from last year's Sherry Recipe Contest. He will prepare the gala banquet in the Nob Hill Restaurant on May 18, 1980, honoring prize-winners and featuring their winning dishes.*

Worldwide Distributors: Fromm and Sichel, Inc., San Francisco, California U.S.A.

Reprinted by permission of Fromm and Sichel, Inc.

up. Others that have been around are the National Chicken Cooking Contest, Weight Watchers® Reader Recipe Contest and Christian Brothers Sherry Recipe Contest.

There are monthly contests, the most famous of which is the *Better Homes & Gardens* special-category competitions, and once-in-a-while, contests for canned hams, canned soups, and almost any other kind of food product. There are even contests directed at the man who cooks, notably *Better Homes & Gardens* "He Cooks."

So while other contests are coming and going, cooking contests are forever with us. Once you decide to pursue this endeavor you will find entry blanks jumping out at you with remarkable frequency. Just keep your chef's eye open as you flip through magazines and trudge down supermarket aisles. You will be gathering entry blanks all over the place, and instead of wondering where you will find a contest to enter, you will be worrying about which to enter first.

Bon appétit!

ANATOMY OF A WINNING ENTRY

It was the last day to get an entry into the Pillsbury Bake-Off, some years ago. It was Sunday, a hectic morning in the household of this particular contester. She had to get her children (four of them) off to Sunday School. Clearly no time to cook. But she had that rare ability and talent I spoke of earlier in the chapter. She had already created many recipes and had won many contests. In short, she knew her way around the kitchen.

On this particular last-minute morning, she recalled a review she had read of a cookbook of favorites at the White House. An interesting seafood dish captured her attention because it called for hot mayonnaise which was, at that time, a surprising ingredient. It also contained lobster and shrimp (too expensive!) and crushed potato chips as its topping.

Our contesting cook did some fast figuring. She could

substitute less expensive (especially a dozen or so years ago) canned crabmeat and canned minced clams. A streusel-type topping—not the sweet cake topping but the same crunchy texture—would be nice. So she translated brown sugar, butter and flour to Parmesan cheese, butter and flour.

Now remember, I said she didn't have time to cook, and she didn't. She named her dish *Crab 'N Clam Crisp*, wrote it up, and sent it off. That's right, she never tested it until she had time . . . four days after she submitted it. And when she did she thought it was delicious!

The judges agreed with her and she won a trip to the Bake-Off in San Francisco that year.

Can you tell, by reading the recipe, that it would combine as well as it did?

CRAB 'N CLAM CRISP

Oven: 350°
Six servings

> 2 7½ oz. cans crabmeat, drained and flaked
> 2 7½ oz. cans minced clams, drained
> 1½ cups finely chopped celery
> 1 cup mayonnaise
> ½ cup chopped green pepper
> ¼ cup chopped onion
> 3 tb. PILLSBURY'S BEST flour
> 1 tb. Worcestershire sauce

Combine all ingredients. Pour into greased 2-qt. casserole. Sprinkle evenly with topping. Bake at 350 degrees 35–40 minutes, or until filling is thoroughly heated and topping is golden.

CHEESE-CRISP TOPPING

> 1 cup PILLSBURY'S BEST flour
> 3 tb. grated Parmesan cheese
> ¼ tsp. salt
> ¼ cup butter

Combine flour, cheese and salt in mixing bowl. Cut in butter until mixture resembles coarse cornmeal.

The nicest part, for me, was being invited to lunch, along with other contesting friends, to sample this recipe and hear all about the trip to the Bake-Off. It came soon after we had all been invited to sample another winner's entry in the National Chicken Cooking Contest, a pistachio-nut-coated chicken. (Part of the fun of this hobby is knowing other contesters; a good part of the fun is knowing contesters who cook.)

I once invited the whole bunch here for lunch, too, and served SWANSON Frozen Chicken Pot Pies. Before you tsk! tsk! I'd like to point out that SWANSON was running a contest, and I not only served the pot pies but put the label from each pie next to each plate. So everyone went home with a qualifier.

A public confession: In case anyone wants to invite me to lunch, I'd rather have *Crab 'N Clam Crisp* or *Pistachio Chicken* than go home with a qualifier from a frozen pot pie.

YOUR TURN—ANSWERS

2. TUNAPPLE TEASIES
3. TUNAMATO CASSEROLE
4. CINNAMINCE CIDER BUNS
5. APPLE DAPPLE PUDDING
6. TEEN BEAN BAKE

And now it's really *Your Turn*. Create a new dish this very day.

8

A Mixed Bag

If you've read this far and have yet to find *the* contest to set your blood pumping and brain cells popping (though I can't imagine such a thing), don't despair, *Your* contest might be here in this mixed bag, an assortment of competitions lumped together, not because they don't deserve chapters of their own, but because some are scarce, some are locals, and some are simply too specialized. But all are worthy of your attention.

Have you wondered if there were contests to write one-liners and where I would bring them up? Yes . . . and in Chapter 8.

Do you like writing statements but are the kind of writer whose note to the teacher about a child's absence tends to run into a twenty-volume set? No matter. There are contests tailored just for you—contests that encourage you to speak your piece in twenty-five words . . . *or more!* There are statements calling for fifty words; one hundred words; unlimited words.

Although the contests in this chapter will be new to you, much of the advice will be the same old stuff: Obey the rules, employ devices, be unique, don't be obscure.

But you're in for a few surprises, too, so don't skip any words.

WORDS! WORDS! WORDS!
(FIFTY-WORD STATEMENTS)

Ah, at last we can use words more or less freely. How nice to write more than one sentence, to use periods instead of dots, exclamations points instead of dashes. How pleasurable to write rhymes in perfect meter and not have to go back and cut beats while bowing to word limitations.

That's the first reaction to a contest calling for fifty words.

The second is: Darn! I wish I could use fifty-one!

Actually, fifty-word statements are fun. They are not drastically different from their shorter relatives, which you've already mastered. It's comforting to be able to use old techniques with new freedom.

A word (or more) of caution: That freedom does not *automatically* include using more than one sentence, since some rules will still specify that you *Finish this sentence* . . . But you will also find many that don't. Read the rules; interpret the meaning. If it says *Tell us in fifty words or less why you like WHATEVER*, you have no lead-in and no sentence completion instruction. But if the rules say *Complete this statement in fifty words or less* . . . and then give the well-known lead-in: *I like WHATEVER because* . . . , you are simply dealing with an overgrown twenty-five worder. But don't worry. You can still write fifty words in the single-sentence structure without sounding like you misplaced the period on your typewriter. I've done it many times and always do so when there is a lead-in.

Some judges, especially in local competitions, are more lenient about this rule. But I always feel that if I'm going to lose, I'd rather it be because I was bested, not ousted.

Don't look for the *Winner Sanctum* at the end of this chapter; there won't be one. Instead, I will give winning entries after each new category taken up. It will be less confusing that way.

LET'S START WITH FIFTY-WORD STATEMENT WINNERS

A single-sentence winner: *I'd like to take my husband to [Rome] because ...*

I'd like him to show me the people and places; explain their concepts and customs, and introduce me to his wartime locale, enabling me to fully understand and partially share memories which, till now, have been singularly his.

Comment: This plain, simple, straightforward entry reads well despite its single-sentence structure. It was different enough and sincere enough, though not especially sparkling, which was why it pulled in a very small prize—some good LPs—but a winner, nonetheless.

Much more to my liking was this fifty-word rhymed statement: *I would like to win AMERICAN FINN OUTBOARD SKIFF because ...*

> *My place in the fun would be assured*
> *The moment I found myself aboard;*
> *Away from the highways and vehicles stalling;*
> *Away from the house with the visitors calling;*
> *Away I would go, out to sea with a grin—*
> *All "ANGER'S AWAY" with AMERICAN FINN.*

Comment: The rhyme reads so smoothly you don't realize it's fifty words in one sentence. A nice parody in that last line adds to the effectiveness of the verse. It won some terrific theater tickets.

An entry packed with sales points, analogy, alliteration and a sloganlike ending, also done in one sentence: *I prefer IVORY SNOW because ...*

... effectively employing the old-fashioned sudsing and safe, pure soap needed to keep delicate lingerie, lovely wools and all family wash close-up clean and fluffed-up soft, Ivory Snow was "born" to "baby" the fabric while beating the dirt, giving all our washables that important "IVORY LEAGUE" look.

No comment—except that the book of nursery rhymes it won was great.

The following entry was written in two sentences even though there was a lead-in. But this was a local contest, and that does make a difference. The contester used her own family name in the entry, which gave it the extra added attraction of the personalization discussed in an earlier chapter—same contester, too.

I would like to vacation at MONTAUK MANOR with my husband because . . .

. . . last year a foxy stork delivered "doubles"—making four little Smiths. I'd feel like Cinderella, substituting MONTAUK for BABY TALK, chasing FINS instead of TWINS.

Comment: Worthy of my mention, and your attention, this was a fifty-word statement contest, but the writer used only twenty-six words to tell her tale. But what words! She knew what she wanted to say (four children; twins; a need to get away), and she went right ahead and said it, briefly, beautifully and sincerely. Who could deny her a vacation? Not the judge of this contest.

By the way, she mentioned her plight with humor. A whining entry about being saddled with kids, and baby talk, and the rest would not appeal to anyone, judges included. Remember that when you're writing up your own tales of woe.

An example of a fifty-word rhymed acrostic needs very little additional comment because it obviously had so much going for it. The "Button" referred to is Dick Button, the ice skater who appeared on the show:

I liked "Hans Brinker and the Silver Skates" on Channel 4 because . . .

Hans Brinker
And sister Trinka—
Never so charming before—
Songs were sweet!

> *Button was neat'*
> *Revealing jumps and spins galore!*
> *It was simply delightful;*
> *Never dull; always bright-full;*
> *Kept tuned until very last minute;*
> *Ended too fast;*
> *Really wished it would last;*
>   *In short; it had everything in it.*

This is exactly how the entry was presented, and it won two great record albums.

Many times the longer statements don't have any kind of lead-in and in that case, no question about it, write as many sentences as you want. ORANGE CRUSH did not give a lead-in; they simply set up a theme: *How OR-ANGE CRUSH helps me make magic as a hostess.* This is total freedom because you can start out any way you choose. And I chose to do it in one sentence . . . but please, don't ask me why.

How ORANGE CRUSH helps me make magic as a hostess: I proudly watch guests' expressions happily change from questioning curiosity with first little sip, to unquestionable delight with second big swallow, whenever I serve Crush 'N Berry Punch, an exhilarating, bright-tasting combination of Crush, cranberry juice, orange juice and frozen berries . . . another Crush way to conquer "party-fare-fatigue."

Comment: Loaded with devices—Contrast, Alliteration, Coined Phrase, even a recipe. The product had to be called "Crush" to stay within the word limit, which was a risky thing to do. But perhaps the nickname added an extra touch, gave it a familiarity-with-the-product kind of flavor. (It's always easy to explain why *after* you've won. In this case the prize was an electric can opener.)

As you can see, all of these statements are nothing more than extensions of the twenty-five worders, so when you come across them, don't panic. Go back to statements, review the how-to, renew the confidence and tackle the job. Prepare as if you were writing a short statement, then luxuriate in the extra words at your disposal. Don't be afraid of it.

HOW TO BE FEARLESS
WHEN FACING ONE HUNDRED WORDS

One hundred words? That's an entry blank full. Frankly, there aren't too many of this ilk around because they're either shorter, or very much longer, like letters and essays. But when it comes to statements, the one-hundred worder is just about tops.

Good news: You don't have to write it in one sentence. At least, I've never seen one with such a stipulation, and if one did exist, I'm glad I missed it.

Again, a statement is a statement is a statement. All the devices that have applied up to now are once again included here. The following winner proves it, and does it so delightfully. I won't say another word except to explain the contest which, in this case, takes some explaining.

Skouras Theatres ran the contest in conjunction with the showing of the movie *Gypsy*. The contest was slightly unusual with Part I a quiz, and Part II a tie-breaking statement. You had to have the right answers to the quiz or you would not be asked to submit a statement. And you had to have seen the movie or you'd never have the right answers to the quiz. There were some contesters who saw *Gypsy* six, seven, eight times—just to get answers to questions like: How many lights were around the makeup mirror in Gypsy's dressing room? What was the year and make of the car they drove? And don't forget, they still had to come up with those one hundred terrific words . . . which this contester did to win a major prize of a HONDA motorcycle.

Why I enjoyed seeing Gypsy: "Want to see Gypsy?" My husband's question <u>planted the seed</u> that <u>grew</u> into a "reel" <u>garden</u> of delightful entertainment. Sitting in the darkened theater, far from my mundane world of dishes, diapers and dungarees, I was swept into that <u>rainbow</u> era of vaudeville. "I" was Louise, the boy-clad <u>sprout</u> suddenly <u>blossoming</u> into Gypsy, the <u>long-stemmed beauty</u>. Rosalind Russell was "my" domineering, driving mother, Rose Hovick—dedicated to a dream. I abhorred her—and adored her. Surrounded by <u>sunny</u> "technicolors," <u>showered</u> with songs, climaxed with Rose's "scenesational" closing number—my evening with Gypsy couldn't miss "<u>Coming Up Roses!</u>"

Comment: The garden analogy was so perfect with the character "Rose" and the "Coming Up Roses" song, and the word limit (or lack of it!) permitted the analogy to be spread around. In a shorter statement, the analogous phrases would bunch up and overwhelm the material—and the judges.

WHEN THERE IS NO LIMIT TO WHAT YOU CAN DO

We come now to one of the few contests that literally has no limit when it comes to words—letter-writing. That is not the only difference between statements and letter-writing. The letter format is an open sesame for you to open up. Because you are writing a letter, you can tell more about yourself, your problems, your solutions than you can in any statement, no matter how wordy.

A good letter-writing technique is to imagine you are writing to one person, not to a sponsoring company or a judging agency. You are telling a story to a person who is actively listening.

Caution: Don't get so involved in that theory that you forget you are competing in a contest. You want your letter to be sincere enough to be believed, but different enough to be noticed. Herewith, one of those examples —a very lengthy one, I might add. The contest called for a "love letter" to a company marketing dog food, and this letter won a few cases of it:

Write a love letter to HILL'S

Dear Sir:

About a year ago I "inherited" a dog. He wasn't very appealing; rather lazy with an "old man" attitude toward life and people. But my neighbor was moving; couldn't take his dog; and offered him to me with the advice that I could "use any dog food; even the cheapest." I weakened when my children pleaded, argued and cajoled. And suddenly I was a "dog mother" with much to learn.

Like any new mother, I sought advice . . . which vet? what food? how much exercise? I noticed one outstanding fact. The people with the nicest, brightest dogs used Hill's Dog Food. The others mentioned various, less expensive, but highly advertised brands. One man even said, with pride, "We give him what *we* eat," but his dog was not very impressive and I soon learned that "our food" creates a completely unbalanced canine diet.

I decided to try Hill's for a while and started him on the frozen horse meat; varied it with canned chopped horse meat; your canned "Dog Food," and (when I could find it) your "Special Pack." The first time Casey had his Hill's he sniffed a little disbelievingly, like a man who, having eaten dried cereal all his life, had just discovered filet mignon. First he tasted; then he devoured; and it wasn't long before Hill's and I uncovered a new dog-personality.

Did I call him lazy, an "old man"? Why, he has the pep of a pup; the eye of enthusiasm, the sheen of a show dog. I would no longer consider a home without a lively, loving Hill-fed dog, than I would have considered buying a dog a year ago. But of course, that was before I discovered that a pet is so much fun; and that feeding him a diet of proper nutrition is so easy and effective with Hill's.

Most sincerely,

(PRIZE: 48 cans of dog food.)

Comment: The letter was subtly "contesty" even though it was a sincerely told story. Knowledge of the product was proved by the mention of the various kinds, even to bringing in the fact that one was hard-to-find. I knew that for a fact because I had trouble getting it, and the honesty in the letter showed itself very clearly. Alliteration entered in an unobtrusive way: pep of a pup, the eye of enthusiasm; the sheen of a show dog. I could have written it to anybody if I were writing about my dog. Maybe it was a bit "literary," but not outrageously so.

It's important to remember, when entering letter-writing contests, that you *may* go on at length, but you must retain the reader's interest. You want him to care, so you won't let yourself bore him; you want him to feel what you felt so you won't be unemotional; and you want to keep him reading, so you won't be repetitive. No matter that you don't have to limit your words—say what you have to say, say it well, and be done with it.

That's all there is to letter writing.

Very truly yours,

P.S. Start practicing by writing interesting, sparkling, lively letters to family and friends. Forget the "I am fine; how are you" approach to correspondence. The more you write, the easier it comes. And writing is what contesting is all about, anyhow.

PERIODICALLY CHECK THE PERIODICALS

For a really enjoyable contesting time, be sure to get into the habit of working on the "fun" contests which abound in magazines and newspapers, sometimes regularly, sometimes as a one-shot deal, always entertaining. They're what we call "quickies"—short deadlines, fast results, and your name in print within a month or two. Several magazines have been running them for years. You'll find a few listed at the end of this section.

Before I get into some specific competitions, I'd like to give you some general tips for all:
• Not necessary to key since winning entries are printed, so you'll know what won.

- If the rules say one entry, send one entry (that's basic).
- Make a study of past winners; reading weekly or monthly winners regularly will be a better lesson than I can give here.
- Keep entering; the more you do, the better you become, and you're working on your hobby.
- If you see the same winning names over and over, be encouraged, not discouraged; it means they're judging fairly and not trying to pick someone new for the sake of picking someone new; work harder and others might get tired of seeing *your* name soon.
- Be neat; type or print clearly; if plain paper is allowed, don't settle for any old scrap; judges deserve a decent piece of paper, if not your reverence and awe (speaking as a judge, of course).
- Don't skip it because the prizes may be small; get into the spirit and you'll find yourself yearning for even an Honorable Mention.

And now, the competitions, please . . .

Playboy

Although known for other delights, *Playboy* surprised us when they ran their First Annual Humor Competition in the August 1978 issue. Since they called this the "First," a "Second" must be planned, so keep watching, especially around the same time of year.

The contests consisted of several sections with cartoon gag-lines, and one-liners. One-liners are something you have the knack for . . . or you haven't. I thought I did. I entered. I found I didn't.

Now it's *Your Turn* to find out if you can write them. Work yours up, then read my losers, followed by *Playboy*'s winners.

Before you start, bear in mind that one-liners are just that—one line that socks it to you (although they can actually be two lines; it's the brevity that counts, not the structure). All the humor is tightly contained. You know, the Henny Youngman school of zingers.

All right. Take my test. Please!

YOUR TURN

1. *It was so hot . . .*

2. *My wife is so fat . . .*

3. *My secretary is so busty . . .*

4. *My girlfriend is so dumb . . .*

5. *His breath is so bad . . .*

My entries were so bad that . . . oh, forget it . . . here they are.

MY LOSERS

1. *It was so hot* in New York City last week it became known as The Big Apple Pie.
2. *My wife is so fat* she was the only witness to an automobile accident, and the papers reported that a crowd had gathered.
3. *My secretary is so busty* she enters a room five minutes before she gets there.
4. *My girlfriend is so dumb* she went to work in a bikini because she was in the secretarial pool.
5. *His breath is so bad* that the only time you can get near him is *after* he's had Shrimp Scampi.

THEIR WINNERS

ONE-LINERS, PART TWO

In which you were asked to complete the following one-liners: 1. IT WAS SO HOT . . . ; 2. MY WIFE IS SO FAT . . . ; 3. MY SECRETARY IS SO BUSTY . . . ; 4. MY GIRLFRIEND IS SO DUMB . . . ; 5. HIS BREATH IS SO BAD. . . .

IT WAS SO HOT . . .
that I saw a fire hydrant flagging down a dog for relief.

Jeff Kwit
Chicago, Illinois

MY WIFE IS SO FAT . . .

she was once arrested for unlawful assembly.

> Mark Schenker and Fred Cohen
> Brooklyn, New York

MY SECRETARY IS SO BUSTY . . .

when she goes braless, her hairline moves forward six inches.

> Terry Miller
> La Porte, Indiana

MY GIRLFRIEND IS SO DUMB . . .

she thinks hair pie is a German mathematician.

> John Sherman
> San Francisco, California

HIS BREATH IS SO BAD . . .

his dentist tells him to say "Mmmmm."

> Michael Marn
> Skokie, Illinois

Games Magazine

Games runs interesting and unusual contests in every issue (bi-monthly, which is every other month, in case you can't keep bi- and semi-monthly straight, like I can't). Some are of the puzzle and number type, and at least one is a creative competition.

I'm not going to tell you anything at all about the two contests that follow. Just as you did in the one called *A Flag on the Play,* pretend you've just turned the page, and here they are. Enter all of them; you know what they say about practice:

YOUR TURN—GREETINGS

A GAMES MAGAZINE CONTEST

Greetings

Grand Prize: Webster's Third New International Dictionary, 2,663-page unabridged edition.

Four Individual Prizes: The Greeting Card Writer's Handbook.

Meet the poor, bewildered editor of the "If You Care A Lot Send Something Else" Greeting Card Co. He's in deep trouble because his entire creative staff went out to lunch and never came back. They left him holding the bag (of unfinished cards) and now he's turning to you for help. Two of the cards were half done and only needed inside messages. A third was designated "Valentine" but nothing was written for it. And a fourth was as blank as the editor's mind. Actually it

was that fourth card that drove the creative department to split. It seems the editor had asked for something new, fresh, different. Something that had never been done before; something like:

CONGRATULATIONS ON LEARNING THE METRIC SYSTEM...
NOW YOU CAN TAKE ME TO YOUR LITER
or
SO YOU HAD QUADRUPLETS...
WELL, FOUR
CRYING OUT LOUD!

As you can see from the samples below, the harried editor struggled to

complete Cards 1, 2, and 3 but he wasn't happy with the results, and he never did get to Card 4. And now it's up to you to help him out. The object of this contest is to write inside messages for Cards 1 and 2 following their opening lines; write a complete (outside and inside) Valentine for Card 3; and/or create a new occasion and write a complete message for Card 4. You may do any one, or as many as all four. Prizes will be awarded for the card we like best in each group, with a Grand Prize for the one we consider the best of the bunch. There is no word limit, but remember what the bard said about brevity being the soul of wit. And the decision of the judges is final.

—Gloria Rosenthal

Clip or copy coupon and mail to: Greetings! GAMES Magazine, 515 Madison Avenue, New York, NY 10022. Entries must be received by October 2, 1978.

1. BIRTHDAY
I CAN TELL IT'S YOUR BIRTHDAY BECAUSE...
(sample) THE GLOW FROM YOUR CANDLES WARMS MY HEART...AND HEATS UP THE HOUSE.

(your line) _____

2. GET WELL
YOUR DOCTOR SAYS YOU GOT TO HIM IN THE NICK OF TIME...
(sample) HIS CAR PAYMENT WAS ABOUT DUE.

(your line) _____

3. VALENTINE
(sample) THERE'S NOTHING NEW ABOUT TRANSPLANTS...I GAVE MY HEART TO YOU A LONG TIME AGO.
(your lines)
outside _____

inside _____

4. YOUR CREATION
occasion _____

outside _____

inside _____

Name _____ Street Address _____

City _____ State _____ Zip _____

Reprinted from Games *magazine. Copyright © 1978 by Games Publications.*

WORKSHEET:

1. *Birthday:*
   I can tell it's your birthday because . . .

2. *Get Well:*
   Your doctor says you got to him in the nick of time . . .

3. *Valentine:*

4. *Your Creation:*

YOUR TURN—GETTING TO KNOW YOU

A Games Contest

Getting To Know You

Grand Prize: Our artist paints your portrait.
Four Honorable Mention Prizes:
Complete Rhyming Dictionary by Clement Wood.

What's in a name? Everything, if you handle it right; and it's your name we're talking about. Just by introducing yourself to us you may gain fame (very fleeting) and fortune (very slight). And considering how forthright we've been in telling you who we are (page 4), there's no reason for you to be shy.

The introduction we're after is, however, a little unusual. What we want is a rhymed acrostic in which the first letter of each line, reading vertically downwards, spells your name and the verse tells us something about yourself.

The following nineteenth-century example may amuse you, and get you warmed up for the competition. It was one of over two hundred acrostics published in *Dick's Original Album-Verses and Acrostics* in 1879, a book that enabled any gentleman to send his loved one a personalized tribute.

> **H**ere is a name which, read it as you may,
> **A** similar sweetness shows from either way.
> **N**o hardness there, no syllable to hiss,
> **N**o guttural sounds ring horrible in this;
> **A**nd so its owner—scan her as you may,
> **H**er charms the same rare excellence display.

For a contemporary example, the editors cajoled me into writing this acrostic about myself:

> **G**orgeous, sexy, tall and slim;
> **L**ovely, charming, full of vim;
> **O**wl-like, stays up half the night
> **R**eading, writing—very bright!
> **I**ndeed she likes to rhapsodize;
> **A**nd also tells a lot of lies!

Now it's your turn. You may use your first *or* last name, *or* a nickname, but please use only one name. Choose any rhyme scheme you like. There is no minimum or maximum number of lines, but you must use one line for each letter of your name. The Grand Prize will go to the entry we enjoy the most, and there will be four runners-up. Please type or print your entry on a separate sheet of paper and be sure to attach it to an entry blank.—Gloria Rosenthal

---

Clip or copy this coupon, attach it to your entry, and mail to: **Getting to Know You, GAMES Magazine, 515 Madison Avenue, New York, New York 10022.**

Name_____

Address_____

City_____

State_____ Zip_____

Entries must be received by April 2, 1979. Each entry must be mailed in a separate envelope, and the envelope must contain *only* the entry and entry blank. All entries become the exclusive property of GAMES. No submissions will be returned. Void where prohibited by law.

Reprinted from Games *magazine. Copyright* © *1979 by Playboy Enterprises.*

WORKSHEET

Did you enjoy working those out? Weren't they a lot of fun? And did you happen to notice who created them?

The same person judged them, and you will find the results in the *Your Turn—Answers* section, at the end of the chapter.

New York magazine

The competition in *New York* is highly sophisticated, well done and well entered. It is almost a status symbol around these parts to get even an Honorable Mention. The magazine is a weekly; the competitions run in two out of three issues, with a very short deadline time. Many of the contests are of the one-liner variety; some are verses, daffynitions, fractured English, and the like. If you're not a regular reader, some of the winning entries will go over your head. That's because a winner might make reference to a competition from a year ago, or refer to consistent winners by name. It's a very "in" kind of thing.

Two of my own Honorable Mentions: *An example of hyperbole:* L.I.R.R.—a commuter railroad running a daily schedule of trains eastbound, westbound, and strikebound. *Redefining of any word beginning with the letter "C":* CORUSCATING: the big finale of the Ice Capades.

A ROUND-UP OF MAGAZINES RUNNING REGULAR CONTESTS

Playboy—watch for contest in Summer of 1980
Games magazine—every issue (bi-monthly)
New York magazine—two out of three issues
Saturday Evening Post—picture-captioning in every issue (nine issues a year)
Omni—every issue; unusual and challenging competitions with futuristic, science fiction flavor (monthly)

Your local newspapers may carry a feature called *Wordy Gurdy,* which is a game you may know under another name. In my childhood it was called—if you'll pardon the expression—*Stinky Pinky* (a "stinky pinky" being the rhymed definition of "odoriferous digit"). They pay $10.00 (don't scoff; it's postage money) for every one accepted for publication. If you can't find it locally, you may submit to:

> Wordy Gurdy
> Public Service
> Newsday
> Long Island, NY 11747

How's this for a Wordy Gurdy? A very smart contester— BRIGHTER WRITER

If you're interested in *Games* magazine and are having trouble finding it on the newsstands, you might want to subscribe. I highly recommend it (no! not because I'm a Contributing Editor and Contest Administrator). It's not just a magazine that runs *a* contest, it is a magazine devoted to contests, adult games, puzzles, tests and features most contesters are interested in. To sucribe for 1 year (6 issues), send $5.97 to GAMES, P.O. Box 10147, Des Moines, Iowa 50349

While we're on the subject of postage money, don't overlook "pen money" fillers like: household hints, embarrassing moments, bright sayings of children, and more.

An example of *bright sayings,* this won a prize for me in an Art Linkletter contest years ago:

> "Don't interrupt when we're talking," Daddy warned Amy.
> "I'm not interrupting," she explained. "I'm talking in your spaces."

This example is given for a very good reason. You *know* what household hints are; you *know* what embarrassing moments are; you also know what bright sayings are, but since I mentioned Edward's "feet fingers" in the book, I wanted to give Amy equal time. (It's my book; I can do that).

As soon as you make your first small sale, be it 10 or 25 dollars, it would be wise to put in a supply of stamps and be ready for the "biggies" when they come along. I'm listing some of these "filler" markets here, but it makes sense for you to check each magazine before submitting, since editorial needs change from time to time.

PET STORIES: Pet Editor
True Confessions
215 Lexington Avenue
New York, NY 10016

True Story Pet Editor
215 Lexington Avenue
New York, NY 10016

VARIOUS MATERIAL: Women Are Wonderful
True Story
215 Lexington Avenue
New York, NY 10016

HOUSEHOLD HINTS: Around the House
Good Housekeeping
959 Eighth Avenue
New York, NY 10019

Also see *The National Enquirer* for current features paying 5, 10, 25, 100 dollars and more. Their needs change constantly, but there are several reader-solicitations in every issue. Worth a look.

ANATOMY OF A WINNING ENTRY

In memory of my mother, Lillian K. Weiss

Mother loved hearing about the prizes Babe and I won and she always insisted on hearing the entries (although nobody ever really had to beg; we were eager to show off, my sister and I). We spurred her on and she decided to get in on the fun by writing a rhymed letter to Babe to which Babe replied:

> *With this new talent you display,*
> *Please enter contests for some pay;*
> *Win trips or cash, or maybe mink;*
> *That sure would put you in the pink.*

Mother picked up the gauntlet—and the pen—and entered a one-hundred worder sponsored by SABENA Airlines and UNITED ARTISTS. Instead of a statement, she used her newly discovered rhyming talents.

I would like to fly SABENA to Paris where Paris Holiday *was filmed because . . .*

> *I have been to Paris; twice, I should say;*
> *Would now like to travel the Sabena way—*
> *Have lost valued time going by ship;*
> *Flying would mean a superior trip.*
> *Business woman that I am,*
> *Time's precious, and I have to cram*
> *Lots of pleasure into each vacation;*
> *And Sabena has no luxury ration.*
> *When speaking of Paris, I melt away*
> *To see scenes pictured in* Paris Holiday.
> *I'd be very gay and act continental;*
> *The fun would be fabulous; my joy—*
> *monumental.*
> *At movie-making U.A. is tops;*
> *While Sabena leads in Atlantic hops.*

If you analyze it along with me, you'll see how cleverly the writer (thanks, Mom) brought in the joint sponsorship, giving them equal time. She also added the nice twist of admitting she'd been there twice by ship, and now she didn't want to waste time. Remember when I said that you might be able to get away with the slightly forced "holiday" rhyme? This is a perfect example of it. It wasn't ideal but it didn't stop the judges from giving the entry 100 dollars, and giving Mother something to crow about for the next twenty years. It was her first contest and she quit after that. So she had the distinction of having won *every* contest she ever entered.

Mother was proud of her entry, and I'm even prouder having it in my book.

YOUR TURN—RESULTS
(FROM PAGES 185 AND 189)

GREETINGS!

That bewildered editor of the "If You Care A Lot Send Something Else" Greeting Card Company can now rest easy. If you entered the Greetings! contest (September/October, page 59), then count yourself among those who helped solve his problem.

The Grand Prize-winning entry written by Miles Klein of E. Brunswick, NJ, in the Original Occasion category, was: Congratulations on your being cloned . . .

Now you'll really know what it feels like to be beside yourself.

Miles will receive *Webster's Third*.

Winning entries in the individual categories were:

1. *Birthday Card:* I can tell it's your birthday because . . .

I saw you erasing your birth certificate again.

Dan Jackson, Indianapolis, IN

2. *Get Well Card:* Your doctor says you got to him in the nick of time . . .

The hailstorm destroyed his roof, and he needed your "shingles."

Marian Desch, Cheyenne, WY

3. *Valentine:* Our love will stand the test of time, and all other tests which true love must pass . . .

Who is this guy Wassermann, anyway?

Dan Crawford, Manchester, IA

4. (Original Occasion) *Apology for dialing a wrong number:* Sorry I called your number by mistake in the middle of the night . . .

Does that mean you won't deliver the pizza?
Lola Schancer, Valley Stream, NY

All will receive a copy of *The Greeting Card Writer's Handbook.*

Congratulations. And thanks for making the "If You Care A Lot Send Something Else" Company what it is today.

—*Contest administered by Gloria Rosenthal.*

GETTING TO KNOW YOU

WE GOT TO KNOW YOU
. . . 3,000 OF YOU

We "met" more than 3,000 of you—from ages 7 to 97—via our "Getting to Know You" Contest (March/April, page 60). Your rhymed acrostic entries ran the gamut from self-praise to self-parody, and were full of passions, foibles, and pet peeves. Artist Lynn Groskinsky will paint the portrait of Ronald Dell (Newton Square, PA) for his Grand Prize winning entry:

> **R**ed-eyed, fat, mean and hairy,
> **O**rnery, growling, downright scary:
> **N**ow that's my wife. Now here is me:
> **A** jolly, handsome reverie,
> **L**ovely, generous, kind and sweet,
> **D**amnably humble from head to feet.

Honorable Mention Prizes of *The Complete Rhyming Dictionary* go to:

Gary Scheel, Staatsburg, NY

> **S**eptember born on Sunday noon way back in
>   Thirty Nine,
> **C**anines were my first love, and givin' Ma a
>   "line,"
> **H**igh School in the fifties with girls of golden
>   hair,
> **E**nter Uncle Sam, Berlin and Cuba, "Drawin'
>   to a Pair,"
> **E**nchanting little children and, of course, a
>   loving wife;
> **L**oquacity be damned, my friend: Six lines
>   about my life.

Jack Shubert, St. Louis, MO

> **J**ust consider my plight—a limerick lover,
> **A**nd christened with letters insufficient to
>   cover!
> **C**ondone in my case
>   (—not a line, just a space—)
> **K**nowing fault's not with me, but with
>   Mother.

Hank Schwab, Chicago, IL

> **H**ello there friends: My name is Hank,
> **A**nd that's my legal name—I'm frank;
> **N**ot Henry, since this is too formal;
> **K**now me: The casual is normal.

Tony Levin, New York, NY

> **T**he truble with me is my speling's the pits,
> **O**n this I'm not sure of the rools of the game;
> **N**ow don't get upset if I've erred a few bits,
> **I**n fact, I'm afrade I have mispelt my name.

—Gloria Rosenthal

9

And If By Chance...

Chance is the key word in this chapter, devoted to those huge fantasy fulfillers: sweepstakes and lotteries. Of all the contests described in this book, this is the type that you, the contester, will have the least amount of control over. In skill contests, the factors that will make you a consistent winner, in order of importance, are: your ability and effort, your persistence, and perhaps some luck like your entry not getting lost in the mail. In sweeps and lotteries, luck plays the starring role, with persistence playing a secondary (but important) part, and ability only brought into play sometimes. (We'll talk about those times later on.)

On the other hand, sweeps and lotteries take very little effort to enter, and in the case of sweeps, very little expense. And there are winners—big winners—who claim that Lady or Lord Luck can be courted with a certain amount of success. The claims run the gamut from sure-fire systems to some apparently logical ways to give luck a nudge. We'll examine the statements of all of our big winners to separate what might really increase your chances from what works only if you're lucky to begin with.

BUT FIRST—CHAPTER 1 REVISITED

There's no way to win any contest unless you get into the game—or in this case drum—and stay there until it's time for the judges to pull out the winner. Remember all those rules back in Chapter 1? It's been a long time, and could be it's time for a little review.

There are some very strict rules, set down by the government, in running of sweepstakes. Since lotteries are illegal except those run by state governments, you may be wondering how come sweepstakes are legal. There is an important difference between lotteries and sweepstakes. A lottery consists of prize, chance, and consideration (the consideration being the money that changes hands in exchange for the "chance"). In a sweeps, it is not required that you pay for the privilege of having the "chance" to win the "prize" so "consideration" is missing. That's why you are always invited to enter national-brands sweepstakes with an alternative to the label or a box top, usually the 3 x 5 inch piece of paper with product name printed on it, for example. That is also why your NO entry has as much of a chance as somebody else's YES entry when magazine subscriptions and merchandise orders are solicited in conjunction with the sweeps. After the orders are processed, the "yesses" and "nos" are on equal footing, and the order, or lack of it, cannot effect the outcome.

Just make sure you follow the rest of the rules, and then check the box you choose. Sorry I'm still throwing those rule-following gibes at you, but the stories I hear about people who *would* have won 10,000 dollars if only they had enclosed a label or alternative; or if only their name and address had been printed; or . . . but you get the idea. And in a minute you will hear one true horror tale that should have you following the rules forever.

And now anticipating your questions . . .

WHY DO THEY CHOOSE SWEEPS?

The benefit to the advertiser is more than the single sale an entrant would be forced to make in a skill contest. It's the entire promotion from newspaper and television ads to store displays and, consequently, to consumer awareness. Besides that, so many more people enter sweeps than skill contests, and many of those do buy the product, so that most judging agencies and sponsors consider sweeps a better promotion. You may have noticed a recent trend to include "cents-off" coupons with entry blanks. That way everyone comes out ahead.

HOW COME THEY WANT HAND PRINTING?

Most of the judges I spoke to cleared this puzzler up for me. They are trying to weed out entrants who have access to computers and company postage meters; in other words, people who can send thousands of entries to one promotion with no effort or expense. Hand printing takes care of that. If somebody wants to hand print thirty entries, fine. But if someone is allowed to send in four thousand mechanically produced entries—well! The nice part of all this is that the judges are not trying to make it tougher on the average person but on those who would be able to have an unfair advantage. So when it comes to the hand-printing rule, don't be annoyed; be overjoyed. It's for your benefit.

WHAT ARE BLOCK LETTERS?

BLOCK   LETTERS

Either style is acceptable.

WHAT IS A RANDOM DRAWING?

A random drawing means that a sampling of entries is randomly drawn from each and every mail bag that comes in. Those that are selected are then placed in the drum for the final drawing. It must be done this way because it would be impossible to have a drum large enough to hold all the entries ... and I'd like to know how they could be "stirred up" if there were such a drum. Judges who do the final drawing from the drum are blindfolded and, in at least one major agency, also gloved to prevent any tactile sensation. The entries are mixed and picked.

WHY DO SOME AGENCIES LIMIT ENVELOPE SIZE?

Only to be fair. Even a blindfolded judge might fall upon an oversized envelope because of the larger surface. Some books on winning sweepstakes advise oversized, even colored or decorated envelopes, and it might help in the random drawing. But more and more agencies are including rules about envelope size.

I like that. In skill contests, the best written entry should win. When it's a matter of luck, it should be the luckiest—not the largest or most colorful.

WHAT HAPPENS AT THE MOMENT OF TRUTH?

The entries are picked, opened and read and, to the shame of about 25 percent of the entrants, that many will be discarded and others drawn from the drum. Why?
- Names and/or addresses could not be read or were left off altogether.
- Qualifiers, or alternatives, were not included.

Sweepstakes, Benson & Hedges style.

100 sweepstakes...and the stakes are yours to choose.

Will you go for 100 hours in Transylvania? 100 pairs of argyle socks? 100 inches of Ford Mustang Ghia? Maybe you have a taste for gold, 100 grams of it...or 100 gallons of sour cream. Or one of our 95 other prizes.

You can even change your mind at the last minute, and opt for 100 feet of dollar bills ($200) in exchange for any prize you win.

Enter as often as you want. Just remember, enter only one sweepstakes per envelope, with the number of that sweepstakes marked in the lower left corner.

This year's 100 sweepstakes has an especially winning look. It just might have you saying, *"B&H, I like your style."*

A pick-the-category-of-prizes sweeps

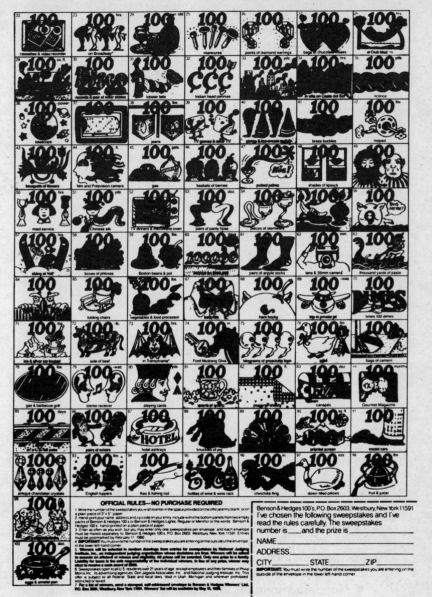

- Information requested on blank was omitted.
- And silly oversights like that.

One judge told me they had picked a 10,000-dollar winner which was discarded because the entrant had failed to include the label or the product name on a 3 x 5 piece of paper. He's lucky in one way; he'll never know he came this close!

There is another reason some entries are disqualified, and it has to do with sweepstakes being illegal in certain states. Although most states are becoming more lenient, if you live in one that is excluded or suspect you're not eligible (if it's for an alcoholic beverage and you live in a state where it's restricted, for example), you can find out for sure by calling the attorney general's office in your own state. You will get better information there than if you call the sponsor.

AN ASSORTMENT OF SWEEPS

The "name-and-address-on-the-blank-and-mail-it-in" sweeps is not the only kind. Some do inject a bit of problem solving or observation or just good guessing into the game. Here are some varieties you may have seen—or will see now that you will be looking for them:

- *Guess the number* of (anything—from the amount of fuel saved by using a new type oil burner to the number of advertising pages in a given magazine); you can't get into the drawing unless you have the right answer, but after that, it is a drawing—and a sweeps after all.
- *Pick the category* of prizes you want to be eligible for. Categories in which prizes are smaller draw fewer entries, thereby increasing your chance to win, and if you do, you'll kick yourself for not having tried for the grand prize, which you probably wouldn't have won anyway because of the greater number of entries.
- *Match the number,* match the name, match the exact wording on the label, store display or entry blank. If you have the right "match" you win. If not, you get a second chance to win by sending your name and address, which

will end up in the sack, barrel or whatever—from which the winner is drawn.

• *Answer the questions about the product*—like what year did it make its first appearance, etc. Once you've found the right answer, you're in the barrel, but you still need luck to have the judge pick your entry out of it.

• *Solve the mystery, problem, game.* Sometimes a company will set up a game or situation, giving clues, rules, etc., by which the clever contestant must come up with the right answer before being eligible for the drawing. These are fun, and while the pick of the draw determines the winner as it does in any sweeps, sometimes, if the game or problem is clever or hard enough, that right answer increases your chances because the wrong answer eliminates much of the competition. You'll see how it works in a minute, when it gets to be *Your Turn* ...

BIG WINNERS AND SUPER SYSTEMS

Some of the winners I spoke to swore by their systems, while others admitted they had none at all, and still more gave some commonsense advice about increasing your chances. Here is a short roundup of the most common kinds of advice, with a little bit of analysis to go with each.

• *Send lots of entries*—as many as you care to spend time and postage for. This is about the soundest advice anyone can give you about sweeps. The more you enter, the more you increase the odds of your getting picked, and if that sounds simple and like no system at all, well that's just the way it is with sweeps—all a matter of odds and luck. And luck still plays a key role. There are grand-prize sweeps winners who've had a single entry, but most of the people I spoke with said they'd sent more than one. One man who's been very lucky (trips and cash recently) told me he usually sends ten to fifteen entries, with no special system of mailing.

• *Mail entries, a few at a time, at the beginning, middle and end of the sweeps.* Some people use this system because of the way entries are chosen. As I mentioned earlier, contenders are picked a few at a time from different mail bags, and mailing at different times puts you into lots of bags. However, as one winner pointed out, if you have lots of entries in one mail bag, your chances of getting pulled out of it also increase. Instinct—and nothing more than that—had most of our contesters feeling you should spread out the mailings.

• *Mail from different parts of town, or better yet, from different parts of the country.* The reasoning is the same as above—the more mail bags you get into, the better your chances of getting picked. On the other hand, the more entries you have in a single mail bag, the better your chances of getting picked out of that one. But the real point is, if you're going to play the sweeps, they should cost you no more than the postage you can easily afford or the time to print those cards with block letters. In games where luck turns out to be the major factor, getting into the game with the least amount of expense and effort is quite enough, especially when there's no guarantee that this trick will help anyway.

• *Play sweeps during off-seasons, when folks don't have much time to enter contests.* According to one knowledgeable contester, there are times when even the hardiest contenders simply do not have time to devote to contests—mostly the summer months, June through early September, and the two weeks preceding and following Christmas. I can't absolutely vouch for the statistics, but it might be worth a try—unless, of course, you're so busy you can't play either.

• *Play sweeps that are prohibited in a lot of states, such as those sponsored by manufacturers of alcoholic beverages.* As I've told you before, you should check out every contest to make sure you're eligible in terms of where you're located. When it comes to sweeps and you are eligible, it might pay to find out who isn't. If a particular sweeps is prohibited in more than an average number of states—it will usually say so on the entry blank— your chances of winning are increased because your competition has been cut down. I used alcoholic beverages as an example because sweeps sponsored by liquor companies are prohibited in quite a few states.

● *Play sweeps that don't get much publicity.* A surprising number of big-money-and-prize sweeps don't seem to get much play on television or in newspapers or magazines which, again, cuts down on the competition and increases your odds. So how can you find out about them?

● *Subscribe to one of the good contesters' bulletins.* Recently, Roger and Carolyn Tyndall's *Contest News-Letter* reported that a very high percentage of their subscribers were winners—often big winners— in sweeps. The statistics were incredible—too much so to be a matter of simple luck. But it wasn't magic, either. The truth of the matter is that the newsletter kept serious contesters informed about all manner of sweeps, even those not so well publicized. A good contesters' bulletin might even tell you which contests are not so well publicized, are prohibited in certain states, etc.

Another word of caution. Some publications will promise to show you how to win a sweepstakes. They'll give you all sorts of advice about calling attention to your entry—by mailing in a larger envelope, or a heavier one, or some such trick. Don't you believe it. Sweepstakes are getting very strict about uniform mailings for everyone. All you're likely to do is break a rule and get yourself disqualified. There's only one way to win a sweeps: Enter often, increase your odds as much as you can, and hope for the best.

● *Play sweeps that require some sort of game-playing ability or creative skill to get into the drawing.* One of the reasons more people enter sweeps rather than skill contests is because they take so little time and trouble. Just fill in the blanks, or print up a card, and mail. But sweeps that require good guessing or problem-solving ability—and the right answers to get into the drawing— are more trouble than some people care to go through. Sometimes they just write down anything at all, or they

Pia Zadora for Dubonnet.

Win 100,000 French Francs!

The French idea of a fortune from the French idea of a cocktail.

Enter the Dubonnet Sweepstakes! You may be the lucky winner of the first prize of 100,000 French francs—about $23,900. And if you're just a little lucky, you could win one of 500 second prizes: a copy of Pia's classic French beret.

Official Rules: NO PURCHASE NECESSARY 1. To enter clearly print your name address city state zip code and the answer to the question "In what year was Dubonnet first made?" This answer may be found by looking at the label on any bottle of Dubonnet A label may be obtained by sending a stamped, self-addressed envelope to: Dubonnet, P.O. Box 21, New York, NY 10046. 2. Enter as often as you wish but each entry must be mailed separately to Dubonnet "Paris Originals" P.O. Box 9, New York, NY 10046. Entries must be postmarked no later than December 15 1979 and received by January 1 1980. 3. Winners will be determined in random drawings from among all correctly answered entries received under the supervision of Marden-Kane, Inc. an independent judging organization whose decisions are final. All prizes will be awarded and winners will be notified by mail. 4. FIRST PRIZE 100,000 French Francs. Valued at approximately $23,900 market value as of April 16, 1979 SECOND PRIZE: One of 500 beautiful Pia Zadora classic imported French berets. 5. Prizes are nontransferable. There is no substitution for prizes offered. Odds of winning are determined by the number of eligible entries received. Local, state and federal taxes, if any, are the sole responsibility of the prize winners based on rate of exchange on the date of award. 6. Sweepstakes open to residents of the United States. Employees and their families of Schenley Industries, their advertising agencies, liquor and wine wholesalers and retailers, Marden-Kane Wesco Associates and Pia Zadora are not eligible. Contest void in Ohio, Calif., Kan., Ky., Okla., Tex., Pa., Ala., Miss. and wherever prohibited by law. All federal, state and local laws and regulations apply. 7. ENTRANTS MUST BE OF LEGAL DRINKING AGE UNDER THE LAWS OF THEIR HOME STATE. 8. For a list of winners, send a stamped self-addressed envelope to "Paris Originals" Winners List P.O. Box 83 New York NY 10046 by December 31, 1979. No purchase necessary.

Dubonnet "Paris Originals" Sweepstakes,
P.O. Box 9, New York, NY 10046

Just look at the label on any bottle of Dubonnet and clearly fill out the entry blank with your name and address, and you'll be eligible for the big "Paris Originals" prize.

In what year was Dubonnet first made?_____
I certify that I am of legal drinking age under the laws of my home state
PLEASE PRINT

NAME_____

ADDRESS_____

CITY_____STATE_____ZIP_____
No purchase necessary See Official Rules to left

DUBONNET APERITIF WINE. PRODUCT OF U.S.A. © 1979 DUBONNET CO., N.Y., N.Y.

Reprinted by permission of SCHENLEY Imports Co., a division of SCHENLEY Affiliated Brands, Corp.

simply don't enter. Again, you're cutting down the odds against you, which brings us to . . .

WHEN THEY WANT MORE THAN YOUR NAME AND ADDRESS

As mentioned in our *Assortment of Sweeps,* there are various types in which you must, indeed, "do something" before you can be considered for the drawing, and you must do it right. True, some of the games or questions may seem very simple, but there will always be a percentage of careless contestants who get the answers wrong, thereby increasing your chances of becoming a winner. The trick here is for you to be careful, observant, persevering, and maybe a little bit clever. As an example, here's what happened when I decided to enter the Dubonnet "Paris Originals" sweeps.

The rules, as you can see from the entry blank, were very clear: You had to include the year Dubonnet was first made; and they told you the date could be found on the label. You didn't have to buy the product; it was possible to send to the company for a label or go into any liquor store and look at the label.

I had a bottle in the house and looked at the label. There was no date. I looked again—front, back, neck label. Even the top of the cap. No date. Frustration time! I was about to call the judging agency and ask what was going on when it was brainstorm time. No reputable sponsor would lie. It *had* to be there and I had to find it. A magnifying glass did it. There is a small bottle of Dubonnet pictured on the label. The small bottle has a label, and the date is on *that* label. I showed the bottle to two other people to see if they could find the date without the magnifying glass. They couldn't. But it was there. And, as I said, it *had* to be.

By the way, the winner in this contest owns a farm with her husband in upstate New York. She found both the contest and the answer in *Contest Newsletter.* This

Entry blank reprinted through the courtesy of the D. L. Blair Corporation.

was her first contest, and like a good sweeps player, she entered often—twenty-seven times.

What do we learn from all this? We learn to be extra-careful, observant and clever. And we learn to believe in the rules.

Caution, again: When the rules tell you to put the correct answer *on* the envelope, put the correct answer *on* the envelope. The judges do not have to open every one to find correct answers as long as they've told you to put it on the outside. And if you haven't, where will you be? Right, *out* of the drum.

For a glimpse of a really intriguing sweeps and an opportunity for you to take *Your Turn,* study this BEEFEATER "Who took the Crown Jewel of England?" mystery-story sweepstakes. I won't say another word about it. You've just come across it in a magazine, and now it's . . .

YOUR TURN

Who took the Crown Jewel of England?

Answer_____

You'll find the solution on page 212.

GETTING SERIOUS ABOUT THE WHOLE THING

There are two ways of looking at sweeps: as a part of your contesting hobby, in which case you'll be spending a certain amount of money on it, or as an adventure in gambling (as calculated an adventure as you can make it), in which case you'll also be expected to spend some money. However, since the motto of every contester is to gain—not spend—you should limit the amount any sweeps will cost you.

Remember those "pen money" items I mentioned earlier—the fillers for magazines and newspapers—household hints, bright sayings, most embarrassing moments?

Well, that could be your way of financing your sweeps career. If you get 10 dollars for an "embarrassing moment," take the money, buy stamps and stationery needs, and gamble the whole thing on one great sweeps with *prizes you like* (be selective). Maybe your "embarrassing moment" will turn into a "thrilling moment."

GOING ABOUT IT THE METHODICAL WÁY

Get yourself some 3 x 5 pads or unruled index cards. Keep them in a handy place with pens, envelopes, stamps, etc., your tools of the trade. A clipboard should be a part of your gear. Next time there seems to be a good sweepstakes going, don't start filling out the cards or addressing the envelopes between lunch for the kids and an appointment with the doctor. Do it while you're watching TV. You can probably get them all done during a couple of nights of just commercials—and then mail them out according to your system. One word to the wise. Since this is largely a game of luck, go only for the contests that offer things you really want. If all the prizes in one sweeps are sewing machines and patterns, and you feel that on a scale of great to terrible, sewing is an activity rated just below having major surgery, then skip that sweeps. On the other hand, if the sight of all that camping equipment flips you out, go get 'em. You can always sell prizes, of course, but there's nothing as exciting as winning the thing you've always wanted.

YOUR TURN—ANSWERS

Who took the Crown Jewel of England? *You* did. When you cut out the entry blank, you took the bottle of BEEFEATER gin that was on it. Notice that BEEFEATER gin is called the Crown Jewel of England in the story and on the blank.

Also notice the wording in the last paragraph: who

takes the Crown Jewel; and on the entry blank, who *took* the etc.

So, after you cut it out you *took* it. A further clue is of course in that last paragraph where *you* are not above suspicion.

Any answer that is not a wrong one (the butler, Lady Trumbull, etc.) would qualify your entry as long as it was clear you understood the premise. You could have said: the reader; I did; everybody who drinks BEEFEATER; you could have given your own name; you could have said "The Entrant." As long as you understood that it wasn't any one person in the room, and your answer made that clear, you did get into the drum.

Of course, it's still a sweeps, but I think this one gathered more incorrect answers than any other. It was more complex than most.

And more fun!

A LOT ABOUT LOTTERIES

Actually, there's not a lot anyone can tell you about lotteries, but what contester could resist that alliterative title. The thing about lotteries is that they are almost exactly like straight sweepstakes—with no side skills in the game at all. And the same principles apply: You can increase your chances by buying many tickets (which can get to be very expensive since they cost more than mere postage), or you can buy your one ticket and trust to luck. Both methods have worked for some people, lucky people, of course.

There was a family in the Northeast, who took all of their savings, hocked their house and valuables—everything—to buy tickets in the New Jersey State Lottery on the off-chance they could increase their odds enough to win a million-dollar grand prize—and they did. But no matter how they shortened the odds against themselves, they still had a good chance of losing—and losing everything. It is not a method I would recommend to any but the most dedicated gambler, and very few contesters fall into that category. There are better ways to come up winning—in a skill contest, for example.

That doesn't mean you shouldn't enter lotteries at all. A contest is a contest, and if it's your hobby, you can afford to invest a bit on the luck of the draw. Again, take the 10-dollar pin money you earn in some small contest, and save that for your lottery investment. Ten dollars can still buy a lot of tickets. And the proceeds from state-run lotteries—the only ongoing lotteries I know of that are legal—usually go to pay for some sort of state service like education, so you can even feel like you're paying for something good while taking your moderate gamble. And by the way, if you think the only way to win is the way that New Jersey family did, lots of other families have lost their shirts that way. Or if you've been listening to "sure-fire" systems that say luck isn't involved, or have elaborate schemes about not buying another ticket after a win, or going to a different dealer, town or community for the next ticket, here's a story about someone who does believe in luck, and in buying another ticket . . . and another . . . and another . . .

It all began during the second month of the New York State Lottery. A very nice grandfather decided to buy five lottery tickets, one for each of his grandchildren. He hadn't learned—yet—that the more names you put on *one* ticket, the better the tax break.

Newspapers published the list of winners, and little five-year-old Jodi Levine won 100 dollars. Very nice.

The next day a telegram arrived announcing that little Jodi not only won the hundred, she was picked to go on, possibly all the way up to a million, but with a guarantee of no less than 5,000 dollars.

I won't put you through the suspense that Jodi's family went through, except to say they were told they had Post Position 8, and this lottery would be drawn from the winning horses in one particular week of thoroughbred racing. Jodi's father, Gerald Levine, checked the charts.

Number 8 won that week about 50 percent of the time. Not bad.

When the final drawing was held, the whole family plus assorted friends gathered at the assigned place and waited. If the third race on Wednesday was drawn, Jodie would be the winner.

Big finish: The first race on Wednesday was drawn, and Jodi was the winner of—ready for this?—ONE HUNDRED THOUSAND DOLLARS. It looks like this: $100,000.00.

The following month another ticket was purchased in Jodi's name, even though they had now learned about the tax structure. Five thousand dollars this time. The odds against this happening were twenty-four million to one. Jodi was picked as a model for the State Lottery, and for an ad campaign then being run by Braniff Airlines: "If you've got it, flaunt it." And she was paid standard models' fees.

Wait! It's not over yet. Every ticket bought by the Levine family after that was purchased in multiple names ...*except* ... you guessed it, Jodi. She always had her own. She subsequently won 100, 100 and 500 dollars in that order, and only on the tickets made out to her, exclusively. Now that is Luck.

Nice ending: Jerry Levine, who believes in sharing his luck, gave out lottery tickets every time a customer bought an Oldsmobile from him at Town & Country Motors in Woodmere, L.I. There were twenty-six small winners and one 5,000-dollar winner among his customers. The big winner paid off her car on the spot.

So lotteries do strike twice ... and thrice ... and on ... and up.

It can happen here! But like the Levine family, you're smart if you play moderately—and don't count on it.

By the way—we bought a car from Jerry, received a lottery ticket and—guess what!—we didn't win a thing.

Lotteries vary from state to state, and even from month to month within a state, making it impractical to give you any real information which could be outdated by the time you get to the end of this page. I'd suggest you write to your State Lottery Commission if you want specific information. They are usually located in the state's capital but may have offices in large cities. Telephone Information can help you locate them.

If you simply want to buy a lottery ticket, you don't have to know a great deal about it. Find a sign that says LOTTERY TICKETS, go in and buy one. The rules and regulations are on the ticket.

Incidentally, buying lottery tickets as token gifts can be fun. Instead of giving someone 5 or 10 dollars (such as a Christmas gift to your hairdresser) give 5 or 10 dollars worth of lottery tickets. Everyone loves them.

I do it from time to time. The only problem I might have some day is . . . how well will I handle it if the ticket *I* bought for someone *else* wins ONE MILLION DOLLARS?

It's something to think about.

10

"I'll Be the Judge of That"

I've just changed hats. This is a "judge" speaking. You know that old adage about a teacher learning from her students. Well, a contester learns from judging. That's kind of what I've been telling you throughout this book —put yourself in the judge's seat. I'm going to put you there in just a little while. But now for my job as a judge, which I got because I was such an experienced contester.

The first time I saw FOUR THOUSAND entries I was tempted to *take two aspirins and CULL them in the morning.* But I must admit that judging entries—at least those submitted to *Games*—is as much fun as entering contests. I enjoy reading entries from all over the country, and out of it, too. Surprised to see that contesters from Canada and England duplicate ideas (some, verbatim) as well as contesters in all of our fifty states.

There were other surprises, too. If I had to guess, before judging, the amount of ineligible entries—entries without name and address, late (very!) arriving entries, and those not following the rules—I would have been on the low side. On the other hand, the quality of the entries was higher than I expected. What a delight!

Although a poorly presented entry would not be discarded for that reason alone—at least, not in a *Games* contest—your entries should be clear, legible (certainly!) and written on an adequate piece of paper without

217

crowding. Don't forget, your words, if too crowded, might be misread no matter how fair the judges want to be.

HOW FAIR DO THEY WANT TO BE?

Well, an even bigger surprise, for me, was discovering I *wanted* my contesting friends to win. I found I couldn't be totally impartial when I came across a friend's entry, and I hadn't expected to feel that way at all. *But wait!* Don't panic. I solved the problem and ended up with a solution completely fair to the other entrants and— maybe—the tiniest bit tougher on my friends. The first time it happened I went in to see Michael Donner, the editor, and admitted that I had two students and one friend in the batch of entries I held out to him. I didn't tell him who they were, and he judged the batch himself. I was sorry to see the students go, but glad to see the friend survive. She survived all the way to the final judging (in which four editors besides myself rated the entries). I disqualified myself when it came time to rate my friend's entry. Happy ending: She was one of the runners-up in the greeting-card contest—with absolutely no help from me. And you know what? I *was* glad she won.

GREETINGS!

Speaking of the greeting-card contest, which you should have just finished working on, there were surprises in that contest, too. Duplication. Actually, I'm not surprised anymore when I see duplicated entries when they are repeated *ideas*, but when they are word-for-word "carbon copies," and they're from such diverse places as Florida and Alaska, I'm still amazed. If you had any of the following ideas in your *Greetings*, try again.

1. The birthday card pulled in droves of references to fire department, fire insurance, birthday suit (plain and wrinkled, which I loved), party hats, every variation of

reminders, notes, calendars, phone calls (from mother, aunt, sister), being over the hill, candles sold out, you and cake both lit up, and more.

2. The get well cards had the doctors (nine out of ten of them) out playing golf. The rest were afraid you'd recover without them, had no malpractice insurance, lost their licenses, were out of *patients*, needed the practice. There were all sorts of references to "nick" (in time saves nine; in time will heal; and others of that ilk).

3. The valentine was the weakest category in that most entrants used our example and relied on various versions of transplants, pacemakers, liver, spleen, kidney. And then there were the inevitable *Roses are red*, in more variations than there were entries (or so it seemed). But all were entertaining, nevertheless.

4. Many entries missed the point of an *original* occasion and were about birthdays, Father's Day, graduation, and the like. Divorce showed up a lot, but there are divorce cards on the market now, so they did not qualify as *original*. Surprising repeats: *Games* anniversary (it was in the anniversary issue), silicone injections, kidney stones, vasectomy and a host of unmentionables.

Now that you've read this, it would be a good idea to rework your own, and then read the winners.

GETTING TO KNOW YOU

Getting to know you, of course, carried a different kind of duplication. Since entrants were working with their own names, it was a highly individualized set of entries. There were repeated "themes" showing up in the verses; that is, loving *Games* magazine (normally flattery will get you everywhere, but not this time), hating housework, loving *or* hating your husband or wife, your job, your name.

The surprises in this contest were the age group—7 to 97!—and the, once again, broken rules. Some acrostics were not rhymed, and others used two names although one was clearly specified.

Again, there were so many good ones that picking the winners was not easy. It never is ... because you'd like to give so many more prizes than you have prizes to give.

How did you do with your name? Do you think you would have come out on top? Would your entry have made us laugh as hard as our Grand Prize winner? If you think so, great! I can't wait to hear from you the next time around. Go ahead, make my job tougher by giving me some terrific material to judge. *I love it!*

Are you wondering if I'm still eligible to enter other contests even though I'm a judge, a writer, and am writing a book on contesting? I wondered, too, so I asked the presidents of five judging agencies. They all gave me the same delightful news: If the rules don't exclude professional writers and such, there is nothing to keep me from winning (except my entries, of course!). On the other hand, I won't be entering any *Playboy* competitions anymore. They recently bought *Games* magazine so my work for *Games* would exclude me from the *Playboy* contests.

I hope you are thoroughly convinced of the integrity of judging agencies, sponsors, and the rest of us. Nothing would kill the public's interest in contesting and, consequently, the sponsors who promote them faster than a little hanky-panky.

I've seen life from both sides of the entry blank, and I love what I see.

YOU BE THE JUDGE

Here, wear my hat for a while and take *Your Turn* at judging, as you did before. Of course, you won't be giving prizes, except to yourself in the form of experience which is, as they say, the best teacher.

For each contest you will find one or more losers and at least one winner. If there are several winners, I'll let you know, give you the list of prizes, and then you will have to pick the order in which they won (or didn't win, as the case may be). An interesting exercise, and fun for

you to see how well you can pick the *Win, Place, Show
. . . and No!*

Don't look at the answers, yet. Wait until you get to the
end of the chapter.

1. There were several houses of different architectural
style at the World's Fair (1964), and the entrant had to
select a favorite and tell why in fifty words or less. To
understand the first entry, you must know that the archi-
tect was Edward Stone.

Read the entries and then match them up with the
prizes following the last one in each batch.

Okay, start judging.

The house I like best is   because . . .

a) (Modern) . . . its beauty is a STONE's throw from ge-
nius—bringing indoors OUT with every patio-view-
ing room; outdoors IN with breathtaking functional,
skylighted atrium; utilizing all property area for in-
side-spaciousness while "cornerin" complete out-
side-privacy makes this home STATUSfying—even
on status "thimble"-sized lots.

b) (Contemporary) . . . without sacrificing purpose, point
and comfort for difference of design, the Coble house,
although unique in the extreme, can never become
tiring. With old-fashioned "house sense," timelessly
beautiful furnishings, and indispensably modern con-
veniences, the architects, by their design, have obviously PUT THEMSELVES IN MY SHOES.

c) (Modern) . . . achieving privacy without seclusion,
"togetherness" without intrusion, this excitingly con-
ceived, dramatically created and constructed house
by Edward Stone has more purpose per inch, more
practicality per foot, and more "living beauty" per
courtyard—affords today's modern family the ultimate in comfortable living, in a price range they can
comfortably afford.

PRIZES: $60 worth of wallpaper;
$200 worth of paint;
Nothing.

a) _____ b) _____ c) _____

2. A "cute" and unusual contest to give a football team's mascot a name and write the last *two* lines of a jingle explaining your choice of name. The given lines appear first; then the submitted name and lines follow.

> *To bring luck to my team at the game*
> *I have given the mascot this name*
> *My reason is clear*

a) GOALDILOCKS
> *For when they appear*
> *"Happy Ending" is always their aim.*

b) TICK TACK TOES
> *Opponents will fear*
> *Their tricks, tackles, toe-kicking fame.*

c) KICKNACK
> *When the KICK-off is here*
> *My team's KNACK will lead them to fame.*

One of these won perfume:

a) _____ b) _____ c) _____

3. What we have here is a jackpot: first, second and third place winners, and the inevitable loser. Your work is cut out for you with this one; aren't you glad it's the good, old twenty-five word statement?

I would like Westinghouse appliances in my home because . . .

a) . . . built for beauty, utility, dependability, in today's fashion with "tomorrow's" features, Westinghouse appliances would give me a comfortable home, full of "SERVICE WITH A STYLE."

b) . . . the FULL-TIME job of keeping house would be easier and pleasanter with the help of appliances that operate for years without "taking a break"!

c) ... Westinghouse BECOMES a home with exciting
styling; expert engineering insures safe, economical,
convenient service without frequent servicing—prov-
ing its beauty is MORE than "trim" deep.

d) ... chosen by builders, preferred by buyers, beautiful
Westinghouse appliances, backed by years of "MO-
TORvational research," assure smooth, superior
performance, reducing housekeeping tensions,
increasing housekeeping ease.

    PRIZES: 1st prize—Westinghouse laundry center
              2nd prize—Westinghouse refrigerator
              3rd prize—Westinghouse range

How do you rate them:

a) _____ b) _____ c) _____ d) _____

4. A two-line jingle starting with KOOL-AID (which
means complete freedom with the rhyming word):

a) Kool-Aid, easy-stored; breezy-good, "SLIGHT OF
PRICE"

   Puts MAGIC in meals, all year long, in a thrice.

(Entrant added: Thrice refers to the quick mixing of
Kool-Aid, sugar and water)

b) Kool-Aid's "Kid Approved"—all year round, it's such
fun;

        Kool-Aid's "Mom Approved"—
        and you know that's hard won!

Which won the Gruen Watch?

a) _____ b) _____

5. *Family Circle* ran a contest in which you had the choice of writing about any advertised product from its pages. Twenty-five word statement.

   I like   because . . .

a) Bennett's Fix A Drink (powdered drink mix):
 Those "ice cream bells" don't bother me;
 The trucks can come . . . or go . . .
 A freezer full of "Bennett Pops"
 Saves tempers . . . tears . . . and dough!

b) CHEF BOY-AR-DEE Meatball Stew
 With meat and carrots, "spuds" and peas, it's
  nourishing I know,
 It's quick to fix, and always clicks with children
  ON THE GROW!

c) VITAPOINTE (hair dressing):
 . . . putting softness and manageability back into "roller-roughened" hair, Vitapointe's extra-light, delicate oils protect; control; condition . . . easily making me the "best-tressed girl in town."

One of these won five major appliances: refrigerator, range, dishwasher, washer, dryer. The other two, nothing. Which?

a) _____ b) _____ c) _____

6. DR PEPPER had an unusual lead line in this twenty-five word statement:

Almost everyone who tastes DR PEPPER says, "It's different—I like it" because . . .

a) . . . an exclusive combination of many delicious flavors, Dr Pepper gratifies adult thirst, satisfies teenage sociability, and earns applause as "the blend of a perfect day."

b) . . . as dinosaurs differ from dogs, Dr Pepper differs from undistinguished drinks; its uncommon combination of many fruit flavors creating a "horse of a different cola."

c) . . . distinctively flavorful, deservedly popular, Dr Pepper is the unique drink made by spirited, progressive people who "get funny" with their ads—NOT with their product.

Pick the one that won an RCA phonograph . . . and you will automatically know the two that didn't win a thing.

a) _____ b) _____ c) _____

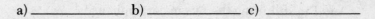

All right, give me back my hat. Your judging chores are over. Don't be discouraged if you didn't do too well. Lots of time we can't pick the winners, but as I've said before, we never know what the competition is.

And now . . .

WILL THE REAL WINNERS PLEASE STAND OUT!

1. a. $60 worth of wallpaper; b. nothing; c. $200 worth of paint.

Comment: These won in the exact order they should have won ("b" was my entry and I hang my head in shame; the others were far superior, but that's not my problem. *I* wrote a twenty-five word sentence-completion in two sentences, and I'll take my twenty lashes with a wet typewriter ribbon).

2. a)—won perfume. I attribute it the name as much as the verse. GOALDILOCKS was a pun-parody, and apt for a football team. The verse wasn't bad, either . . . and probably a much more unusual rhyme than "fame" which was repeated two out of three times right here.

3. (a)—2nd prize—refrigerator; (b)—nil; (c)—1st prize —laundry center; (d)—3rd prize—range.

Reread all the entries. Do you see that the one loser did not say nearly as much as the major prize winners? A good test for a twenty-five word statement is: Does it sound like a lot more? That's usually a pretty good clue that there are no wasted words. All of these winners had lovely Red Mittens and all of us had lovely appliances.

4. (b)—won the watch. Nothing much to say here. It's

really a better entry and didn't need an "addendum" to make it clear.

5. (a)—won the five major appliances. Probably an unduplicated idea; expressed in a nice down-to-earth way in spite of its being in verse. I liked (b) also; was surprised it didn't win *something*.

And I'm still using the five major appliances!

6. (c)—was the only winner in this batch and deservedly so. It said much more than the other two about the drink itself and adds a very nice pat on the back for the sponsor. I loved it; wish I had written it.

How did you do?

11

In Record Time

Now that you know how to create all those terrific entries, you're going to learn how to write them up, write them down, mail them out, collect your prizes and . . . pay your taxes (sorry about that).

I'm an organized person. The magazines in my magazine rack are placed in there alphabetically. Don't scoff. If I'm looking for *Apartment Life* it will be right there behind *American Journal of Nursing, The.* My contest records are equally organized. How else could I have written a book if I didn't have twenty years of entries appropriately filed? It takes no extra effort to begin with and saves lots of effort later on. The methods in this chapter will assure that you don't miss deadlines—and will help you locate any entry you ever wrote, even years from now.

WRITE IT UP

How will your entry look to the first judge reading it? Clearly legible, I hope. Unfortunately, we don't always have as much room as we'd like when an Official Entry Blank is required. It's frustrating to have an OEB apparently designed for six words instead of twenty-five, but that's an occupational hazard. There are some solutions to the problem, none of them terrific.

If typing is permitted, try to use a typewriter with elite type instead of pica type: more characters to the inch. If you're hand printing your entry, do it small enough but *legibly* enough to get it all onto the blank. In the past, I have typed up an entry on a small piece of paper and pasted it onto the entry blank, making sure that what I'm covering up is not important to the entry. (In other words, if your lines are following a lead, or a jingle, don't paste over that portion.) I can't give you "blanket permission" to blanket the entry this way because, I'm told, *some* judges might not approve. As long as it's not covered in the rules, we can't be certain. I use the method only when I'm desperate.

Now, typing, printing, writing, and what's the difference? This, too, can be a question of interpretation.

Carolyn Tyndall (part of the team of Carolyn and Roger Tyndall who put out the *Contest News-Letter,* about which more later) has written a supplement called *Guidelines for Entering Contests and Sweepstakes.* Here is Carolyn's view of this all-important question:*

• When the rules say "print" or "hand-print," you may use block letters or you may use caps and lower case letters. When the rules say "hand written," we recommend that you hand print. After all, printing is a form of writing and it is one of the easier forms of writing to read.

• Do not type your entries unless typing is specifically mentioned in the rules.

• If the rules say "hand address" or "hand print" the address on the envelope, do NOT type. If hand addressing or hand printing the envelope is NOT mentioned, it is our opinion that you may use a typewriter for addressing your entry envelopes.

Carolyn's interpretation is on the cautious side, and that really makes sense, although I have won when I typed entries calling for printing. *Caution:* If they want you to sign the entry, they want your signature in your own unique hand*writing*, not your printing, not your typ-

---

* *Reprinted with permission of Carolyn and Roger Tyndall.*

ing, not even your rubber stamping. There's something so nice and legal about a signature.

I'm a strong believer that *neatness counts* even when it's not mentioned. Compare, in your mind, two entries: one neatly typed or printed; the other a mass of ink blots, smudges, illegible writing plus a coffee stain or two. Case dismissed.

WRITE IT DOWN

You've written it up for the judges; now write it down for your records. I'm going to give you the Rosenthal Super-Duper Record-Keeping System, but you may want to make up your own. That's all right. Just get into the habit of doing it right, and doing it right away. Don't say, "I'll enter it later." You won't.

Equipment (none of it exotic): a three-ring loose-leaf binder (large rings—you're going to have a lot of entries eventually), paper, a batch of 9 x 12-inch manila envelopes, and a hole punch. They're good investments, because you're going to stick with this hobby whole-heartedly and not give up if you lose the first few contests. Right?

Directions: Cut off the top of the manila envelope (including the flap) so it's the right size to fit into your loose-leaf book; cutting just below the metal clasp is about right. Punch three holes on the left side so the envelope will fit your binder:

Now cut a "V" on the front only:

This strange piece will hold all the material you need for each contest: entry blanks, labels, contest bulletins relating to that contest and your own work sheets. Have one envelope for each contest, and write the name of contest and deadline date on each envelope (in pencil so you can erase it and use it again when the contest ends). By putting them in order with the most current contest on top, you can open your book and see at a glance when your next deadline is. Be sure to note whether the deadline is a *received* date or *postmark* date, and file accordingly. *5/31/80 rec'd* would actually be filed *ahead* of *5/25/80 PM* (*postmark*) because it would have to be sent out first.

After the envelopes: Now you have a normal-looking loose-leaf book. Mark the first page PRIZES, and rule it for date, sponsor, prize. This is your permanent record . . . and you can add pages as those prizes mount!

After the PRIZES section: The rest of the book will quickly fill up with entries . . . and never send an entry out without first writing it down in your book. In this section, I write down Name of Contest, Judging Agency, Deadline Date. Under that, I list all my entries and my keying for that contest. When you win a prize, circle the winning entry, write down the prize on the page, and then record it on the PRIZES list.

MAIL IT OUT

This is nothing more than repeated advice to get it out on time. Don't think you can drop your mail into a mailbox on deadline day, and it will surely be postmarked that day. Check the pickups at various boxes. Mailboxes with a star have later pickups; others might have an 11 AM and then nothing till the next day. Get to know the pickups in the various boxes in your neighborhood, or become totally paranoid like I am . . . and run to the post office with everything. You can check the accuracy of a certain box by mailing yourself a letter from that box.

None of these hysterics would be necessary, of course, if you would not wait until the last minute, but that's advice I can't really hand out too freely. Something about the pot calling the kettle late.

COLLECT YOUR PRIZES

I don't mean literally to run around collecting your prizes. I just want to prepare you for the "big ones." For smaller prizes, you will receive a letter of congratulations, and then your prize will be shipped to you. Short of thanking the sponsor (which should *always* be done; they do deserve that), there's not much for you to do but crow a bit. But larger prizes . . . ah! . . . that's another story, and a glorious one.

Affidavits: An affidavit is a beautiful piece of paper which you must sign, attesting to the fact that you wrote the entry yourself; you didn't plagiarize it; you don't work for the sponsor or judging agency; and such. Affidavits must be notarized, and any bank can take care of that for you, although some won't do it if you don't have an account there.

At this point, you will be ecstatic and will be sure you've won a major prize. I'm telling you not to be too overjoyed at this moment, but you won't listen to me anyhow. All contesters have had the experience of getting affidavits, getting excited, and then getting a small prize, or worse, no prize. The reason this happens is that judging agencies must send out more affidavits than prizes to cover themselves for the percentage that will not be returned. (Maybe somebody *did* "steal" an entry, or *does* work for the advertising agency; doing it seemed all right until they had to swear they didn't.) So, most of the time, an affidavit means a big prize, but some of the time it doesn't. I had such an experience with MOJUD hosiery some years ago. I wrote a slogan for a teen-age safety slogan contest—A friend who'll speed is a FIEND indeed—received a letter and affidavit, returned the "affy" (contestese for an affidavit) and then . . . nothing. The following correspondence took place between Mojud and me. I didn't get a prize, but I did get a kick out of the whole thing and never regretted the experience at all.

December 6, 1957

Congratulations:

Your entry in the Mojud Teen-Age Community Safe Driving Contest sponsored by The National Young America Safe Driving Program, has been selected from hundreds of thousands, and is being considered in the final competition. This gives you the opportunity to win one of the grand prizes which will consist of 1958 Fords, T.V. Sets, Polaroid Cameras, and Lucien Picard Watches.

We are enclosing a questionnaire which is being sent to all contestants who are eligible for final judging. We would appreciate having you complete this form and return it to us by December 15th. A return self-addressed envelope is enclosed for your convenience. Final judging will take place the latter part of December and winners will be notified as soon as possible.

With your participation this contest has contributed to the awareness of highway safety among the young people of America.

Very truly yours,
Morris L. Judson
General Sales Manager

ODE TO DISAPPOINTMENT
or
SORE-LOSER'S LAMENT

by Gloria "Sore-Loser" Rosenthal

I'm a sore-head I suppose
'Cause I am mad at Mojud Hose;
They sent me such a cheerful note
I couldn't walk—I had to float;
I wondered what my prize would be—
A car? A watch? Or just TV;
The waiting got me quite annoyed;
I'd settle for the Polaroid.
But nothing came as days went by;
I tried to laugh—alone, I'd cry;
"They have some nerve," I'd say out loud,
"I just can't stand that Mojud crowd."
Oh, I'm not mad at Reuben D.
Those fellows haven't bothered me;
They toss my entries in a basket;
My signature? They never ask it;
My efforts there have not been praised
And so my hopes have not been raised;
But when a letter says "Congrats"
And nothing follows—CURSES! RATS!
My friend, Sue, just won a pony
Which proves that Reuben is no phony
But Mojud's prizes by the dozens
Must have gone to aunts and cousins;
That "Friend who'll speed"—it will be me
As I run on a "strike back" spree
And start a fad to make them sick
They'll wish they hadn't pulled this trick;
They're office safes will need no locks
When I shout:

"GALS! LET'S ALL WEAR SOCKS!"

February 24, 1958

Miss Gloria Rosenthal
144-35 226th Street
Laurelton, New York

Dear Gloria Rosenthal
Who we don't think is a sore loser at all.
If you can write the way you did,
We are sure you haven't blown your lid.

Here is the way it goes, you see
The questionaire? Sent to all who might be
Winners in this contest spectacular,
And honestly we're not using vernacular.

However when final selection was made
Yours was not included we're afraid,
In the one hundred winners they elected
From many more hundreds that were selected.

You understand now, we have no doubt
What winner picking is all about.
Nevertheless, you will be pleased to learn
The Safe Driving Contest indeed did earn

So much enthusiasm on the part of all
Who have interest in safety . . . it was truly a ball.
So thanks for your entry in the contest
and thanks, too, for doing your best.

May we urge you to enter another promotion
Known as Famous Pairs Giveaway which will soon be in
    motion.
Your dealer will have entry blanks, more than less
Which merely require your name and address.

Very truly yours,
Morris L. Judson
General Sales Manager

My reply:
Just because you took the time
To answer my complaint in Rhyme;

A life-long friend you've made of me;
It's Mojud now, exclusively.

If some day you've naught to do;
And want to write a rhyme or two
I'll reply with Deathless Prose
While I am wearing Mojud Hose.

Investigations: Sometimes, when it's *the* prize, an investigator (usually a Burns or Pinkerton detective) will call on you. These visits are nerve-wracking, exciting, bewildering and thrilling. When asked if I've ever won anything, I always answer honestly. Be pleasant, answer all the questions, and in general, be the kind of person the sponsor will be pleased to have win his contest. When I won the first prize in SAKRETE®, I received a call from the president of the company telling me they were surprised, and delighted, to learn a woman had won.

Remember, we want more contests, and we want to be the kind of consumer who will give contesters a good name. We don't want the greedy, complaining sour-grapes kind of person in our ranks.

Sure we want to gloat and crow, and we can. But we should do it in such a way that nobody will hate us!

I hope you will be putting this advice into practice soon—how to handle an investigation, I mean. If I'm going to lose out to you, I want to say, "Okay, I lost to someone who's entry was better than mine, and to someone who's nice. I can take that!"

PAY YOUR TAXES—OR
YOUR UNCLE, THE PARTNER

That's Uncle Sam, of course, and he wants to share in your winnings. All right, I'll wait until you stop gnashing your teeth.

There's no kind way to tell you that you must pay taxes

on prizes. If you win a trip, you have to pay taxes on the amount that would be considered Fair Market Value for that trip.

The Internal Revenue Service defines Fair Market Value for us:

> Fair Market Value represents the price at which the property would change hands between a willing buyer and a willing seller, neither being under any compulsion to buy or sell, and both having reasonable knowledge of all relevant facts. Sales of similar property, on or about the same date, may be helpful in determining Fair Market Value.

Reading that over should convince you that you cannot —legally—sell a 9,000 dollar prize car, let's say, to your daughter for ten dollars and expect to pay taxes on ten dollars. You pay on the market value: on what that 9,000 dollar car would go for at a *reasonble discount* price (nobody pays the sticker price anyway).

I *never* fooled around with taxes, and I'm not saying that just because I'm making these statements in print for all the world—and the IRS—to see.

For prizes you don't sell, you still have to pay the taxes on the Fair Market Value. It is, after all, additional income and is taxed as such.

Bur for all of that, I still want to win 25,000 dollars and will gladly—well, maybe reluctantly—pay the taxes.

12

A Highly Prized Group

Now that you know what contesting is all about, and now that you realize you have the "write" to life, liberty and the pursuit of prizes, and now that you're getting yourself organized, it's time to think about meeting with others of your ilk. That's where NCA comes in.

NATIONAL CONTESTERS ASSOCIATION AND WHY YOU SHOULD JOIN IT

If you've ever belonged to any of those "special interest" clubs or groups (overweights, chess players, campers, photographers, lion tamers, whatever), you know, first of all, how much fun it is to be with people who share your problems or interests, and secondly, how much you can learn from people who share your problems or interests.

Contesting is no different. As a matter of fact, contesting is probably a better example of camaraderie among competitors than almost any other endeavor. If you belong to a photography club, for example, and have competitions—even if you're restricted to, let's say, winter scenes or children at play—your photos will be considerably different from those of other members. But in contesting, everyone is working on the exact same project, all striving to write the best entry, and yet people stand

237

up at conventions and give away all sorts of winning help, explaining how they won in a similar contest and what should be done to make your entry better than your competitor's (sometimes their own).

Sounds crazy? Whoever said contesters were sane?

NCA was founded forty years ago by Everett Lane who still invites contesters to convene annually in Fredricksburg, Virginia, which is only one of many regional conventions.

And then, there's the "big one," the national convention. And it's great!

WHAT'S SO GREAT ABOUT AN NCA CONVENTION?

Everything! All right, I'll be explicit.

The conventions consist of an early bird session (the night before it really gets under way), followed by three days of meetings, a banquet, and a house party (for those who can join together for an extended weekend at a resort). I love the meetings because they are:

- Informative—speeches by judges and contest bulletin editors
- Inspiring: speeches by those big winners who tell you they did it and you can, too (and you know something, you believe them!)
- Stimulating (and unique)—quickie contests are being conducted all day long in the middle of the meetings —five minutes to write a slogan; ten minutes to write a twenty-five worder; or even overnight deadlines ("Entries must be dropped in the box by noon tomorrow"), so you go back to your room with your head spinning out a few choice words, and Morpheus is cheated once again. But it's the best practice in the world.
- Entertaining—because the whole thing is FUN! And you're learning—sometimes even earning—while you play.

SPECIFICALLY SPEAKING OR YOU ARE THERE

The last NCA convention held, as of this writing, was our fortieth anniversary bash at the Philadelphia Sheraton in July, 1979. I was there. And through the magic of print, you're about to be there, too.

About two months before the convention, when you send in your registration fee, you receive what is known as the "Prefab," a booklet containing ten contests. You work on these at home; mail them in by deadline date; and hope you will have some winners in the batch because prizes will be given at the convention. (The prizes are small, but there is nothing like winning among your peers!)

Interesting fact about the Prefabs: each member is assigned a number, and it is your number, not your name, that you put on your entry for identification. It isn't until the winners are announced at the convention that those judging know the winners' identities.

I promised you would "attend" and this is the first step. Here is your Prefab. Try to complete all the contests: no matter how difficult they may seem. It will be fun to compare them with some of the winners at the end of this chapter. Not doing them would be like going to the convention and not participating.

YOUR TURN

(Answers at end of chapter)

LIBERTY BELLES 'N BEAUS

Annual Convention of National Contesters Association
July 15, 16, 17, & 18, 1979
Philadelphia Sheraton
Philadelphia, Pennsylvania

USE ONLY THESE OFFICIAL ENTRY BLANKS. Indicate REGISTRATION NUMBER ONLY on your entries. Registration number is shown on the front of your prefab and on the back of your name badge. Registration badges can be picked up at the convention. TO ENTER THESE CONTESTS, YOUR MEMBERSHIP MUST BE PAID THROUGH JULY, 1979.

Only ONE prize will be awarded to a contestant in any one contest. Cash prizes in each contest are expected to be $20.00 for Stay/Winsiders and $50.00 for Gos, as follows:

1st prize	$15.00	ATTENTION: STAY-AT-HOMES & WIN-SIDERS *ONLY:* Your entries will be judged separately and prizes determined by number registering.
2nd prize	10.00	
3rd prize	5.00	
4th prize	3.00	
5th prize	2.00	
6th–20th each	1.00	

GO's entries must be mailed to person listed on the blank and must be postmarked no later than *JUNE 15.* Same postmark date for Stays and Winsiders. No refunds after June 30th.

CONTEST #1   Registration # _____

If you could have been one of the Belles or Beaus in and around Philadelphia during Colonial Days, whom would you have chosen to be and WHY? 25 words or less. Judged on originality and aptness.

_____

_____

_____

CONTEST #2   Registration # _____

Write a last line to the following limerick:
> If William Penn could join our fun
> He'd change his name to William PUN
> Then 'twould be PUNsylvania
> Hosting our contest mania

_____ .

Rhyme with Pun and Fun. Judged on meter and humor

CONTEST #3   Registration # _____

Begin with any well known "line" of 20 words or less, then write the name of a famous American who MIGHT have said or written it. Judged on aptness and originality.

_____

_____

EXAMPLE: A stitch in time saves nine. Betsy Ross

CONTEST #4   Registration # _____

Write a 4-line jingle, using the following first line. Pick your own rhyme words.

> Sweet BELLES thought Philly BEAUS were great

_____

_____

_____

Judged on rhyme, meter, cleverness

CONTEST #5   Registration # _____

In 15 words or less sloganize in vignette form why a nostalgic Belle or Beau impressed you. Judged on aptness, originality.

_____

_____

Example: Daniel Boone . . . He really moved his TRAIL for you!

CONTEST #6   Registration # _____

If Benjamin Franklin were the present day Editor of the Pennsylvania Gazette what headline would he write to precede the story about NCA's Fortieth Convention? 10 words or less (NCA will count as one word). Judged on cleverness and Franklinese.

_____

_____

CONTEST #7   Registration # _____

Everyone knows the Liberty Bell cracked in 1835, but what they don't know is it was done by an elated contester who wanted to announce he had just won a $25,000 prize. Name the crack in the Liberty Bell in 4 words or less. Judged on originality, aptness and cleverness.

_____

CONTEST #8   Registration # _____

The winter of 1777–1778 that George Washington spent with his men at Valley Forge was bitterly cold. In 15 words or less tell us how COLD was it? Judged on believability.

_____

_____

CONTEST #9   Registration # _____

Many pioneer people had rather quaint names. As a result, weddings often joined together two remarkable "fitting" names. Think up names for such a couple using two words for each name.

_____

EXAMPLES: Shirley Soprano & Drummond Scales
            Daphne Dilly & Lyman Dalley

CONTEST #10   Registration # _____

The famous words of "Give me Liberty, or Give me Death," and others, have gone down in history. In 15 words or less, what famous words have YOU written— and entered in a contest—that may make their mark in history? Could be a line or slogan. Judged on originality and aptness to subject.

_____

_____

Example: WON for all and all for WON.

AT THE CONVENTION

Sunday morning at the Philadelphia Sheraton. We check in, drop our bags in our room, and rush to the convention hall to greet old friends we haven't seen since the last local or regional conventions. But this is the big one—members from all over the country. Hugging, kissing, cries of "Congratulations . . . I heard . . ." Newcomers are swept into the feeling of closeness with people who were only names in the *NCA Bulletin* until now. Here you get to meet someone who, once a novice like you, just returned from a prize trip to Europe, only to find she won a car while she was away.

We buy tour tickets so we can get to touch the Liberty Bell on our free afternoon; we buy banquet tickets so we will be there for the "big dinner," the roll call of states, the entertainment, the installation of officers.

The Early Bird is announced, and it is a revelation to any newcomer and your first introduction to what you will come to call the Quickie Contest. You hear the instructions, but you don't believe it—*five minutes* to write a last line; *ten minutes* to write a 25-word statement! They must be kidding! But there they all are, at rows of long tables, thinking, writing, revising like crazy. Everyone is doing it, so you do, too. What the heck! You do the next one . . . and the next . . . and before the day is out, you will have entered fifteen or twenty Quickie Contests. And you're exhilarated because you've discovered an important truth: The more you write the easier it comes. Maybe you didn't win anything this time around, but you can't wait for the convention to get underway the next morning—and for more of those Quickies.

Monday morning: Official opening of the Fortieth NCS Convention. Words of welcome by our President, Mrs. Marjorie Goldberg, and you really do feel welcomed. Speeches. A discussion about writing verse.

And then . . . a Quickie Contest is announced, and by now you feel comfortable with the pressure. Ten minutes to compose your own "law."

"You know, like Murphy's Law." It's explained. "If anything can go wrong, it will. But this is your own law."

That's a tough one but something comes to me, and I scribble it down just as they're ready to collect the entries:

My law is . . . if I served Braised Octopus Belly for dinner . . . my husband had it for lunch.

While these entries are being judged, some Prefab winners are announced (such good writing!), and then the "law" winners are read. My entry wins first prize, five dollars. What fun!

Monday afternoon: Panel discussion of recipe contests with winners telling how they did it. Not only that, but current contests are discussed, and interpretation of rules in cooking contests turns into an interesting question-and-answer session. Again, I'm impressed with the unselfishness of contesters who discover tips through their own efforts and then pass it on to their own competitors. (Hey! Isn't that what this book is all about?)

Monday evening: Pow Wow is reserved for first-timers. The registration form you mailed to make your reservations had a place for newcomers to make a note that this is their first convention. If you must go to your first convention alone, don't worry. You won't be alone for long. You'll certainly discover this at the Pow Wow where you are made to feel welcome—and almost like an old-timer by the time it's over.

Tuesday: More talks on specific types of contests (always interesting); more Quickies (always fun); more Prefab winners (always suspenseful as you wait to hear your number called).

The afternoon is open for the bus tour of Philly and I do touch the Liberty Bell.

Wednesday is exciting. Local news team arrives at the beginning of the session with lights, mikes, television cameras, the works. And we are on the Evening News. The timing is right. We are able to catch the news right before the Banquet.

Dinner is excellent, but that's the least important part of the Banquet. More winners are announced for contests that had run all during the convention. There had been one to name the Texas Fly (a *huge* model of a fly); another calling for a slogan for the 1980 convention; even one to write a statement about Tabasco Sauce.

I pick up two more prizes at the banquet.

CONTEST: Pick any professional group and supply an appropriate title for a trade journal for that group.
MY ENTRY: Morticians—DEAD LINES

CONTEST: Add your own two lines to this jingle:
    San Diego here we come
    "Write" back where we started from
MY LINES: *Writing entries P.D.Q.*
    Pencils pointed—heads are, too!

Which gives you some idea of the "flavor" of the banquet. All fun and all the entertainment in the same vein. There is a certain joy in the air.

And it continues on to the House Party, which is the NCA name for that portion of the convention that is not a convention anymore, but an extended weekend away with friends. This year it is at a resort in the Amish country, and we spend the next few days doing what every other tourist is doing—seeing the sights, taking the tours, eating the wonderful food—but we are doing it with contesters so the contesting chatter goes on.

Then the sad goodbyes until next year, and we go home determined to work harder than ever on upcoming contests.

If I had to pick my favorite moments of the convention, I couldn't, but if I were "forced" to do so, I'd choose the Quickie Contests. No—the Prefab winners. The speeches? The Banquet?

Oh, what the heck . . .
See you in San Diego in 1980,
And in Charleston, S.C., in 1981.
Start making plans.

NOW THAT YOU KNOW WHY, HERE'S HOW

The convention isn't the only reason for joining NCA. As a member you will receive five *NCA Bulletins* a year which contain all the latest news about NCA members. There are reports on *Winsiders*, (members who are shut-ins and are helped by others who send blanks and labels), news of contest clubs all around the country, and contests and contest announcements in every issue. Plus full reports on regional and local conventions, including transcripts of speeches. All this for six dollars a year. Incredible!

Send your check or money order to Mrs. Carolyn Burnett, 220 Hampton Hall Lane, Conroe, TX 77301.

And welcome to the club!

YOUR TURN—ANSWERS

Prizes in the Prefab contest are all small cash awards, from one to ten dollars. But this is one time the size of the prize is really not as important as the winning. When your number is called and you go up to the "head of the class" (and this group is "class" when it comes to contesting), you don't for a minute believe that "Winning isn't everything." *It's so much fun!*

1. A composite of colonists I would be
   Who fought the "STAMP ACT" ACTively!
2. Wordsmiths forge onWORD, get job done.
3. "Let George do it!" Martha Washington.
4. When Pa allowed his girls to date.
   While they were bundling, she was chaste;
   Just one mistake, then she's disgraced.

5. Francis Scott Key—He put people back on their feet again—and again—and again.

6. RICHARD joins NCA—no longer POOR.

7. AFFIDAV-HIT

8. When a guard shouted "Halt" soldiers froze in their tracks never to move again.

9. Caroline Cotton and Joseph Pickett

10. Make the S.P.C.A. your Pet charity.

13

The Beginning

Did you think you were all through just because you reached the end of the book? I mean, I'm glad you got here, but this is only the beginning. It's the beginning of your new hobby, and it should be the beginning of some new reading habits.

There are times when every hobbyist, no matter what the hobby, loses interest momentarily, maybe needs a little nudge to get him going again. That's why club meetings of all sorts are popular. They remind the members that they really do love their hobby whether they're currently into it or not.

You may not be ready to join a contest club, yet, or perhaps there isn't one in your neighborhood and you're not quite ready to form your own (which is what I did way back when I was starting out). But you are ready to subscribe to a bulletin or two, take a correspondence course, or at the very least, stock your bookshelves with the few important books your hobby cries out for.

Here's the place to get the information.

YOUR MAILMAN AS TEACHER— CORRESPONDENCE COURSES

I've made reference to the Shepherd Contest Course elsewhere in the book, and now I'll fill in the missing pieces; the how, where, and how much (you should know the why by now).

"The Shepherd Course in Contest Winning" is a 12-month correspondence course featuring 75 lessons and 2,000 winning entries to learn from. Cost is 48 dollars at 4 dollars per month, or 40 dollars if paid in full. Free for one year with the course is the *Confidential Contest Bulletin* containing information and winning help for current contests. Bulletin available separately by subscription, 7 dollars for ten issues. Write to Shepherd School, P.O. Box 366, Willingboro, NJ 08046. For sample copy of bulletin send 75 cents.

Glasser Guide to Filler Writing: a roundup of news, views, tips and techniques on how to win contests, create and sell fillers (My Most Embarrassing Moment, etc.). For free details send SASE (self-addressed, stamped envelope) to Selma Glasser, 241 Dahill Road, Brooklyn, NY 11218.

THE BULLETIN BOARD

Here you will find bulletins of every description, some arriving monthly, others being published only when material will fill a bulletin (you pay by number of issues; in this case, not a yearly rate); all contain rules, deadlines and judging information. Some contain winning help for current contests, reports of wins and winning entries, occasional interviews with judging agencies and big winners. Skill contests, sweeps, puzzles, poetry and more are covered. Each has something different to offer. I have my personal favorites; it's up to you to pick yours.

Shepherd Confidential Contest Bulletin: sold separately from course; see course listing for details.

Contest News-Letter: a twelve-page monthly bulletin; $12 for one year; for free sample copy, SASE (business-size envelope) to Roger Tyndall, P.O. Box 1059, Fernandina Beach, FL 32034.

Golden Chances—Dedicated to Better Contesting: one year, $10,00; sample copy 50 cents plus SASE to Tom Lindell, P.O. Box 655, South Pasadena, CA 91030.

Sweepstakes Digest: five issues, $9.50; single copy, $2 to Shirley Brennan, P.O. Box 877, Humble, TX 77338.

Eggleston Enterprize: twelve issues, $6.50; sample copy free for SASE, business-size envelope to Eggleston Enterprize, P.O. Box 2732, Milford, NY 13807.

Ideas, Techniques and Secrets: twelve issues, $8.50; ITS, 31 Woodland Street, M-3, Hartford, CT 06105.

The Prizewinner "The Folksy Contest Magazine": one year, $10.00; one issue, $1.00; The Prizewinner, P.O. Box 10596, St. Petersburg, FL 33733.

Golden Eagle Newsletter: a brand-new publication filling a void in poetry-competition information; five issues, $5.00; twelve issues, $10.00. Box 1314, New Milford, CT 06776.

A CASE FOR BOOKS

Some books are absolutely essential if you are to pursue this hobby in earnest—a good dictionary, rhyming dictionary, thesaurus and a few others that are nice to have and will often spark ideas. Basic to your bookcase:

Analogy Anthology by Selma Glasser (available from Selma Glasser, 241 Dahill Road, Brooklyn NY 11218, $4.59 paperback)

Clement Wood's Complete Rhyming Dictionary or *Wood's New World Unabridged Rhyming Dictionary* (costs more but I prefer it)

Roget's College Thesaurus in Dictionary Form (paperback)

Webster's Unabridged Dictionary, Third Edition (my choice but any good dictionary will do)

These books will get your "library" started; you may want to add more as you go along. Handy books to have around are a pocket-sized rhyming dictionary (available in most bookstores) to take traveling with you; the *Instant Spelling Dictionary* (has a nice roundup of rules of grammar; at your bookstore or Career Institute, Division of Grolier Enterprises, Inc., Sherman Tpke, Danbury, CT 06816.

As I said back there at the head of this chapter:
This is the beginning!

YOUR OWN WINNING ENTRIES

Let your winning entries become a permanent part of this book. This is not meant to take the place of your loose-leaf book, so when you win a contest be sure to enter it in both books. Keep track of the date contest ends (deadline) and the date you receive your "letter of congratulations." It's nice to know how long it takes so you can judge the "waiting time" for future contests, all approximate, of course.

If you keep—or give away—a prize, enter its Fair Market Value. If you sell it, put the selling price in. It's fun, and often surprising, to add this up from time to time.

I hope these pages fill up quickly!

Deadline_____ Sponsor_____
Judging Agency_____ Notification date_____
Prize_____ Value_____

WINNING ENTRY:

Deadline_____ Sponsor_____
Judging Agency_____ Notification date_____
Prize_____ Value_____

WINNING ENTRY:

Deadline_____ Sponsor_____
Judging Agency_____ Notification date_____
Prize_____ Value_____

WINNING ENTRY:

Deadline_____ Sponsor_____
Judging Agency_____ Notification date_____
Prize_____ Value_____

WINNING ENTRY:

ABOUT THE AUTHOR

Gloria Rosenthal's love of words has brought her full circle from contesting (where it all began) to freelance writing, to teaching a course in *Writing to be Published,* to becoming a Contributing Editor and Contest Administrator at *Games* magazine where, to complete the circle, she creates and judges contests. Her articles, humor, light verse, fiction and quizzes show up in a variety of publications including *The Wall Street Journal, McCall's, Good Housekeeping, Reader's Digest, The New York Times, The American Journal of Nursing, Prime Time* and *Playbill,* to name a few. In addition to words, she loves the theater, camping and photography. She works in her office at home on Long Island, but if you ask her to meet you in New York City, she will be on her way before you finish the sentence.